Like Daddy Used To Say

By

Niki Rowe Cross

©2015

Contents

Like Daddy Used to Say....and Others

Few people in this world work as tirelessly and with more vindication in their hearts than Niki Cross and her army of volunteers at the STAAR Ministry. Unfortunately our world today is filled with more problems than solutions, constantly shifting global politics create and destroy communities and allegiances. Cross, however, is not one of those forces. As steady as the North Star, she is a Tsunami of help to women who have had the most unspeakable things done to them, fracturing them as people and from society. Helping close to a 100 women every year STAAR Ministry is an indispensable resource for people who have become victims of 21st Century slavery and forgotten by our social system. Given Florida's dominant role as a port for human traffickers, we don't need just one STAAR Ministry, we need a dozen more people like Cross doing the work she does stitching victims back into the social fabric most of us take for granted.

Michael Bou-Nacklie
International Photojournalist/Fancyhat MultiMedia

By the time Niki Cross finishes what you think will be her story of abuse, addiction, loss, and pain, you realize those may be chapters along the way, but they are not her story. To be sure, her experiences are fundamental to her journey, but the real story is one of redemption, healing, and hope in the person of Jesus Christ, as shared through the down-home wisdom of her Daddy. Niki is a story-teller and putting her book down in the middle of it is no easy task. She takes the reader through some of the harshest and most unimaginable realities of life but somehow leaves us optimistic, determined, hopeful, and inspired to move forward through our own muck and mud to something better.

Brent Woody
Executive Director/Lead Counsel, West Florida Center for Trafficking Advocacy

S.T.A.R. Ministry is the life-line for broken women who want to restore their body, mind, and spirit. The tremendous positive impact of this ministry is driven by an incredibly beautiful woman, Niki Cross. Due to Niki's own experience and hard work, she understands the rawness of the women she serves and passionately seeks to help them become whole.

Dotti Groover-Skipper
CEO, The FREE Network and Founder of HeartDance Foundation

Acknowledgments

How do you possibly acknowledge all those who have in some way been a part of the intricate pattern God used to weave your journey of life? I know some will be missed in name, but you are etched in my heart, and in everything I do that reflects your wisdom and patience. In no particular order, I thank the Pastors who have spoken powerful words that have been part of developing my walk. Howard Kendrick, for loving me when I tried your patience, and for showing me what Godly looks like. Even when I didn't deserve it. You might have wondered if anything you said got through. Like any seed, it took time, but it took. Every day the roots in God's word get stronger. Thank you for showing me the balance of love and correction. Most of all for teaching me Luke 4:18.☺

To Nicky Cruz, for taking time out of a crazy, busy, evangelical ministry, to meet on a Sunday afternoon with an extremely angry teenage girl who wouldn't share the reason for her anger. Who knew we'd one day have the same name (different spellings, different language) in common?

To Mr. Gene Keith, whom I enjoyed talking to so much. Thanks for all your help and encouragement to write this book.

To Billy Joe Daugherty. Thank you for being a living example and although you have gone home, we will meet one day and compare notes.

Dana, my mentor and friend, for being honest and telling me I was full of it. Your honesty probably saved my life!

To Milton, Jack, Betty and Chico. Thank you for watching over me in Nashville, while God was watching me slowly submit.

My longstanding and beautiful childhood friends, Terry and Phyllis. You knew me and loved me, then, as you do now. Thank you for being real friends. For the side splitting laughs that pulled me through, and holding my hand when I literally cried, until I could cry no more. Terry, no one has yet to be a worthy opponent playing Rock Trivia like you. For all the times you and I have "Faced the Nation" together. The times we have spoken entire Beatle's lyrics to have a conversation. We spoke our own language. Phyllis, we only have to be in the same room and it becomes nonstop laughter. The day of the robbery only reminded me how much it would hurt if you were not in my life. Grateful for God's protection over us, and a chance to say I love my friend once more.

Dr. K and Dr. H, for hearing zebras, when everyone else heard horses.

My dear friend Pamela, who showed me how important changing the playground was – and best shopping buddy ever!

To Donna "Danno" Bradshaw. Thank you for all the years you have let me pour out every hurt and frustration, and never judged. For never allowing me to believe anything but victory was an option. Your sweet, sweet spirit is real and infectious to all who know you. I am blessed all the more for knowing you! Love you, friend!

Kate Bennett (Kate Bennett Photography). Your professionalism is second only to your kind and gracious heart. You have honored me, and every survivor who created art from their pain. You literally turned my vision into an artistic reality. Color me grateful!

My precious friends and fellow advocates. Dotti, Jen, Ida, Natasha, Beth, Donna. Oh how many times you have supported me and kept me focused, when others played badly in the sandbox. Your love and loyalty to the cause astounds me. Colleagues that are in law enforcement, you are a joy to work with, and supporting you is an honor. If I listed you all by name I'm afraid there would be little room for anything else.

To my aunts, who know who they are. For always loving me and knowing there was always "more to the story" than me just being a bad kid. Thank you for loving me with mercy and not following the pack.

For Chrissie and Buster, what can I possibly say? I am here because you stepped outside of what was comfortable and easy. For not setting a boundary of who we help simply because "we don't know you." Gratitude doesn't come close. You are the real deal where heroes are concerned. Chrissie, we are forever family and sisters.

Pamela & Brent Woody, and Stan Arthur. All you've done to support not only my ministry, but given to survivors. You are simply amazing and I'm grateful beyond measure.

To John, wherever you are. Buddy, I pray you are free, healed and have peace.

Mama, you have been the most stubborn individual I've ever known. No doubt that is probably what's kept you going. Your determination has helped you jump hurdles most would have said were too hard. Beneath all that armor I know beats a heart that loves fiercely. I will always be your baby.

To my sweet, sweet Daddy. Oh, how I miss your wisdom and how loved I felt by you. I'm so grateful for inheriting what money could never buy; the love of a Daddy that was pure and real. Save a place for me!

To my amazing husband and sweetheart, Peter. Thank you for putting up with my intolerable behavior and seeing something behind it. For being an example of balance and unconditional love, and believing I was worth yours. For allowing me to heal in my time, without ultimatums. Your modesty is most likely causing you to cringe about now! Although you're not perfect, you are perfect for me! I love you.♥

Thank you, my amazing Lord for loving me when I couldn't love myself. For teaching me I don't have to perform, or make promises to be loved. For allowing me to come to know the real Jesus, while also getting to know the real me. For all the times you were so close, leaving no gap between us, that I mistakenly felt alone. I will honor you when others mock, because I know my true survival lies with you. I love you, Lord.

Introduction

I'm so glad the bible says "And it came to pass" instead of "It came to stay". Going through bad times is not what equips us to help others. It's going through those times, taking responsibility when necessary, seeing ourselves honestly, and repenting when needed. Otherwise, we've just become experienced in misery. Forgiveness will not change your past, but it will change your future. We have to decide. Do the trials in life make us bitter, or do they make us better? Playwright and author Fulton Oursler said, "Many of us crucify ourselves between two thieves. Regret for the past, and fear of the future." We've all had pain, but remember…there is always pain right before a delivery. We've all been kissed by a Judas. But remember…right after Judas, came a resurrection.

Forgiving someone is not contingent on whether they change, or even whether they meet our standards. It also does not condone the action. In fact, I often advise we should always forgive, just sometimes from a different address. Tragedies are only tragedies when we refuse to see where God was in the middle of them. There are many reasons for writing a book and not all are honorable. When God put this on my heart, I felt neither capable, nor willing to open all the doors necessary to be completely honest. So there were many watered down versions prior to this. I was determined not to do as I've seen others do, blaming and finger pointing. Character assassinations that come off as one dimensional excuses for bad behavior or poor choices. And yet, I knew to write this as needed, in a way that showed all my flaws, as well as my redemption, would involve some uncomfortable truths.

Many have told their stories with either visible venom or revenge, or as self-righteous heroes. I pray that I have managed to keep the honesty, without others feeling attacked. Truth is truth, and to help others, it must always be present. So, if not for fame or fortune, or thinly veiled as a disguised tactic to hurt those that "had it coming", why? For all that have been, or are headed, down this path, not just as a survivor of abuse, but as someone who wondered why the rest of the world seemed to be part of a club that I could never belong. Never quite fitting in. And yet, the more open and honest I became, the more healing took hold. The more I realized I was not so different, while maintaining I am unique, as are we all to God.

I can truthfully say writing this has not been without struggle. Considering the size of this book, you'd be surprised at the amount of time it took to put it into print. Many old wounds were opened, as well as my frequent hesitations. Although I shared the details with my husband over 17 years ago, and have always had his full unconditional love and support, the stigmas and mindsets of my community and generation would often tempt me to remain silent. I grew up in a time and community when, if an unmarried woman, much less a child, lost their virtue, they were automatically labeled as damaged goods or tainted, and it didn't matter the circumstances. I love my hometown and I am proud of my roots, but I am also well aware of the gossip mills and criticisms that have harshly and unfairly labeled individuals without mercy. There were times when I would attempt to test the waters, trusting people with less explosive truths, but rarely felt complete freedom from ridicule. When we are people pleasers or care more what man thinks than God, it can keep one silent a lifetime.

We are by nature a voyeuristic society. This is why reality TV shows have reached such popularity. Even though they are often staged settings, it sends the message that you are sometimes getting a peek into someone's private life. Gossip has been part of society as long as man has communicated, and it is this fear of being the subject of gossip that gives the enemy so much power, and convinces us to hold secrets. When the threat of exposure is removed, we can focus on the healing more than the hurt.

It was only after I began to minister to women and was able to relate my own hurts that I began to notice something unique happening. The first years of ministering were very often done one on one, in confidence, and with huge gaps of time in between. Regardless of whether I am ministering to one or hundreds, the elements that must always be present are that I share my history and am completely transparent. The common response of "you don't understand" is only then completely removed from the conversation. Those three words have hindered more recoveries, including my own, than any other I know.

Once people realize that someone else has walked a similar journey and survived, there is hope they too can beat the odds.

It was never my desire to open this to the world, but it is my desire to be obedient to God. Even at the expense of pride and judgement.

I cannot preach to those who pretend to be superior and wear prideful masks if I refuse to remove my own.

There are details many will want to know. But I will not sensationalize to simply entertain. I have bared when necessary to show transparency, and also be relatable to those who may need to see where one has walked a similar path. There are names that have been purposely omitted for legal reasons, but mostly to focus on the healing, not the hurt.

How often do we limit the changes and healing that God can bring to our lives? I often think of the woman at the well that interacted with Jesus. In John 4:4 the bible says, "It was necessary for him to go through Samaria." I've often wondered if that was from a geographical need, or because she *needed* him. Either way, there was an encounter, and a lovely example of how little we expect, but are capable of receiving. You see, this woman went to the well only expecting to take home a bucket of water. Instead, she left with a river.

I've taught many, for years, "There's no limit to how much good a man can do, as long as he doesn't care who gets the credit." If that's true of man, why would we *ever* want to suppress the limitless amount of good God can do in *our* lives? Like many of you, God was the *LAST* subject I ever wanted to discuss. I had watched way too many talk what they didn't walk. So I have committed to do what my sweet Daddy taught me, "Preach the Gospel to everyone I know--and once in a while, use words." – Niki C

"Concrete Minds: All Mixed Up and Permanently Set"

When you hear someone say they were born the child of a poor sharecropper, you can't help but wonder if that's just a corny line from a comedic movie. I assure you there is no punch line to follow. Mama and Daddy were the hardest working people I've ever known. Daddy, which is often pronounced more like "Deddy" in the south, would rent the land and the little shell of a house that usually stood somewhere in the middle of the acreage we farmed. While the house would have been, by middle class standards, substandard, it was always clean and tidy. Our diet consisted mostly of beans, potatoes, and biscuits. A heart surgeon's nightmare. But I never remember going to bed hungry. Central heating and air-conditioning would have felt like we'd won the jackpot. So we kept warm by the use of wood and kerosene heaters. Summer heat was only re-circulated by the whirring of fans strategically placed around the house. Looking back, I now see there is a lot of truth when speaking about material things. You don't miss what you've never had.

Farming took up the majority of the year. Planting crops started in early spring, and the work ran into late fall just in time to start back to school. There were never beach trips, camping, or any sort of family vacations while my folks farmed. Neither time nor money was something we ever seemed to have enough of. Daddy used to say, "Why drive two hundred miles just to take a picture standing beside your car, and then turn around and drive back home?" He probably said that to convince us *and* himself that we weren't missing anything. He actually learned to enjoy traveling before he died. In fact, we once visited my sister in Tennessee, took a few pics by the car, and then drove back home.

The work never paused or stopped during the cold months of the year. During the period of time Daddy had livestock, just going out to feed the animals could be brutal. His poor hands stayed chapped, red, and cracked from the cold. Wood needed to be sawed, chopped, and hauled to heat the poorly insulated house to a tolerable warmth. When the cold of winter passed, this meant planting, and the farming started all over again. It was a constant cycle of work to survive.

Mama, like my Daddy, never caught a break either. During crop season she worked just as hard, and pulled her weight, as much as any man they ever hired. I remember her joking about leaving the young guys a bit outdone. My Mama has always had a very competitive nature, but she also knew our very existence depended on what those crops produced. Nothing could be wasted. In the fall, she would head back to her "job in town" as she called it. She had a long standing agreement with her employer. She was a farmer's wife, and when the agricultural side briefly paused, she would then return as cashier, sales assistant and stock clerk at the local dime store. Now we have dollar stores, but in the 1960's a dime would actually buy something besides chewing gum. A family friend once commented she would have to be buried standing up, meaning she never stopped going. She was the original "Energizer Bunny." ©

Mama, as of this writing, is in her eighties, and there's no doubt she's still a Type A personality. When God is not leading those personalities, it often leads to years of feeling unfulfilled. Nothing is ever good enough. No one makes you feel appreciated. It can turn into a vicious cycle that wears you out physically and emotionally. It's only been in recent years that she's started taking some time to enjoy things and not hit the floor running with a mental "to do" list that stretches from one end of the earth to the other. More than likely because of age rather than submission.

Days working at the dime store were long, with very short breaks. She barely had enough time to choke down a sandwich, visit the restroom, and return to the floor. Most of the day was nonstop walking, standing, pricing, and putting out new stock, all the while attending to any customers that may need help, or watching for that matter. More times than few, she would have just finished folding clothing or straightening out merchandise on the shelves, when someone would come right behind her. As if only to torture her, they would wreck her intense organization, requiring her to do the same task she'd only finished minutes before. Unfortunately it seemed she had more of those days than I care to remember. Each time, we would see her as she drove into the yard with a face like thunder we knew we were in for a stormy night.

It was years before I realized you could actually have a conversation without having to yell. It was just as many years before realizing you don't have to walk on eggshells everywhere you go. Until I was nine years old my older sister caught the brunt of it. But I still had to dodge a few verbal bullets of my own. I often say my sister and I were raised in church, but not in Christ. I get why people wouldn't want anything to do with God, based on my early examples. People watch us, and how we behave does matter. It wasn't until I met real Christians, with real hearts for God, that it dawned on me just how backwards I'd been taught. For instance, when Jesus spoke to the woman who was about to be stoned, (John 8:1-11), he forgave her and said to go and sin no more. Somehow, my church interpreted that as, "Go and sin no more and then I'll forgive you." It was an impossible task. Most churches, I believe, have a bit of dyslexia. In Matthew 28:19, Jesus tells the apostles to go and make disciples of all the nations. But somehow that's been turned into, "Go into the world and make "Denomi-nations". I'm convinced they believed Jesus died so they could be "bored again", instead of "born again".

Mama's family had attended our church for generations. Most of the members were extremely bitter and judgmental people. I swear they'd been baptized in lemon juice. I remember a particular Sunday school teacher who was so mean, if she had asked me if I wanted to go to heaven I would have most likely responded, "That depends. Are *you* gonna be there?" We're talking "frozen chosen" extreme. The bar was set so high, no one could live up to their expectations. I'd often hear things like, "Well if you were a Christian you wouldn't act like that", or "wouldn't behave this way" or "wouldn't say that", yet never giving instruction or mentoring on what the right thing to do or say would have been. I was led to believe each time I failed, salvation had never been real and Jesus had not heard my plea. With each and every altar call I signed up for every baptismal. By the time I was thirteen I had been dunked more than a donut. I repeated these steps over and over until it finally sank in. No matter how hard I tried, I would never be good enough. So why try?

This went a long way in crushing my already fractured self-esteem. One thing I have learned is people who judge usually feel judged. I look back at many of the people who were so harsh and critical with their words. I realize their lives were turned upside down at home.

In contrast, this was not a description of my Daddy. Daddy, bless him, was loved by many people. It didn't dawn on me just how much until after he'd passed. One of the officers that escorted the funeral procession said he bet there were at least five miles of cars following. He'd never seen anything like it, except with VIPs. I remember we had to eventually commence with the graveside service, because it was taking so long to park all of the incoming cars. Daddy was not an educated man, but he had more wisdom than some with as many degrees as a thermometer. He had a saying for everything. He was a philosopher in overalls. In fact, you'll hear me say many times "like my Daddy said" for this or that. I've often said he was a walking bumper sticker, and friends tell me the apple hasn't fallen far from the tree.

If I had to describe him physically, he was a cross between Andy Griffith in looks and nature, and Phil Robinson's no nonsense wisdom and staunch faith. I pray in sharing many of my Daddy's words you'll get a good balance of love and laughter in this book. I loved my Daddy so dearly, and felt terrible anger for such a long time after he died. It was only when I stopped concentrating on *WHY* Daddy left, and began to think of *WHAT* he left, that I was able to use his precious treasure of words to help others, as well as myself, move on. I can almost hear him now as he used to say to me, "Let go and let God are not just pretty words, girl. They're instructions." Wounded people often get stuck in behavior patterns. They want to do it their way. This brings to mind a childhood memory. My Mama, my Daddy, and I were riding in the car one day with the radio on. "My Way" came on, the Elvis version. As we rode on listening to the song, out of the blue my Daddy very seriously spoke up and said, "Well I declare, they've done gone and wrote Hell a theme song" giving me a wink in the rear view mirror.

"God Won't Heal What You Don't Reveal"

My sister was nine years older and had been an only child. Just when it looked like it would stay that way, I came screaming into the world, on a Sunday morning in May, at Parkview Hospital in Rocky Mount, North Carolina. Rocky Mount was such a small town back then. I've often joked I was raised in dysfunction junction, zip code AEIOU. There's nothing wrong with being from a small town, just being small minded. The hospital is long gone and the lot is still, for the most part, vacant. However, just across the street stands Thompson Pharmacy, which opened sometime in the 1920's. With the exception of the old nursing dorm, now a part of their parking lot, having a bit of wall paper and a lick of paint, not much has changed. It's one of the few remaining pharmacies with soda fountains that still "serve with a smile." Until you've wandered in on a hot day, sat at the counter, and had a fresh squeezed orangeade or lemonade, it can't be quite appreciated for its historic place in the town. In fact, while many pharmacies across the country have closed their doors with the explosion of chain stores on every corner, Thompson continues on, and will hopefully do so for quite some time to come.

I'm sure my arrival was confusing to my sister. It's hard for any sibling to welcome what is naturally seen by children as rivals. But with reassurance and preparation, children can usually adapt and actually look forward to the new brother or sister. Knowing how Mama probably viewed my conception, as more stress in our house, I have no doubt that very little encouragement was ever given to her. I'm certain in my sister's little mind she wasn't sure whether she should view me as an ally, or the enemy. Over the years, we've been both. With all the pressure of farming, housekeeping, cooking, and a new baby, at some point, whether gradual or immediate, most of these duties, including *me,* fell into my sister's lap. Don't misunderstand me. Children need responsibilities. They need duties, chores, and boundaries. This is biblical. But as I will try to stress throughout this, everything must be done with balance, emotionally, physically, and especially spiritually.

As stated previously, my sister was nine years senior. So when I was three or four, she would have only been twelve or thirteen. I look back and realize she was just a child. And yet to me, she always seemed to be an adult. It's no wonder, with what she carried on her shoulders. When she came home from school and on Saturdays she was the full time, live in, babysitter. She gave me my baths, which she must have dreaded. As a preschooler, I hated baths. I would run and hide in the closets, under the beds, and even once, under the house. I don't know why, as my sister always made the huge kitchen sink look like a giant meringue of suds and I absolutely loved it. I would usually play as long as I could, pleading with pruned little fingers to play a little bit longer. I can remember my sister changing sheets on all the beds. Sweeping, dusting, mopping, doing laundry, and a fair bit of cooking to boot. Back then, it didn't seem to be unusual. But in retrospect, that was an enormous amount of responsibility for a child. I don't know what the alternative would have been, with both of my parents having their own plates full. I mean, she had all that, plus *ME* to deal with! I now have such compassion for her, which eluded me for so long. It has taken God's grace and healing of my selfish thoughts, to be able to see it from her perspective. By the time my sister reached eighteen she took off for greener pastures. Her story is not mine to tell, but there have been many battles, mostly uphill, she's had to fight. My sister is very bright. She has accomplished a great deal, and I admire and love her immensely.

At the time she left, everyone presumed my change in behavior was a direct result, and yes, I was completely devastated by her abrupt leaving. In my mind, it felt as if I'd lost my mother. She was the one who took care of me, for the most part, day to day. We were so close. We even slept in the same bed. I can remember as she drove out of the driveway with her friend I ran so hard trying to catch the car, crying, I fell face down in the sand. I laid there and wept for what felt like an hour, until my Daddy came, picked me up, dusted me off, and brought me back into the house. I do not harbor ill feelings about her departure. But I can tell you, it probably caused a lot of the abandonment issues that took years to overcome. With every friend, every job, every spouse, I was always waiting for the other shoe to drop, and for them to all go away. I also began to self-sabotage. After she left, I made sure from that point on, I'd be the one in charge of who left first.

The master of pain and evil doesn't have any new tricks. He simply changes his window dressing from time to time. He still delivers each blow with pain, making it harder to forget. We remember good things, but not in detail like we do with pain. The area of my life in which I felt most confident was my voice. You'll hear more about my pursuit of music later. For now, I'll tell you singing in elementary school gave me friends. High school - made me slightly popular. As an adult - a budding career in Nashville. When the music stopped, all the ugly memories came back and the feelings of low self-worth flooded in. I was constantly performing, one way or another, to make people like me. I felt if they saw what I was really about they'd want nothing to do with me. It was always a different mask, to hide the real me. I only wanted people to love me and not leave me. I now know with my sister, this was no overnight decision. Children tend to only hear what they think important. The fights between her and my parents were nothing new. So her threats of leaving became a volley ball match back and forth. The day finally came when it was no longer a threat, she was gone. It would take many years and many prayers, for healing between her and my parents. As she was no longer in the home, my father became my primary care giver after school, as well as summer and weekends. Mama was home in the evenings but was usually exhausted from work. At this time my Daddy was still farming and had plenty of work to do. I was sometimes left in the care of different family members.

It was hard enough at nine, losing my sister. To add insult to injury, the molesting by a relative began. I never told my parents, out of shame and fear they would view it as my fault and blame me. The perpetrator was in his teens; therefore I didn't view him as an adult. I was deceived to believe it wasn't abuse. I hadn't stopped it, so it must have been my fault. Remember, in my community bad things didn't happen to good girls. This continued until I began to beg Daddy if he had to go out, "Please let me stay home alone." I would defiantly protest "I'm old enough." I often wonder if I really convinced him I was old enough or if he suspected something and didn't let on.

This person actually kept making attempts to molest and touch me until I was about seventeen years old. He made one last attempt at my paternal grandmother's funeral. By this time I'd become much angrier, as you will later understand. I was also very street smart. So when he tried to touch me in an inappropriate way I made an angry threat. I'm sure he sensed from the look in my eyes I was dead serious. He must have seen the hatred boiling over, because no more attempts were ever made physically. However, I believe his fear that I would tell created a new abuse. I had made so many mistakes by this time, it gave fertile soil for his lies to grow. He was growing into a young man with aspirations for success. Being labeled a pedophile would have restricted his chosen occupation. Years passed, and he became more embedded into the "respectable" community. His lies and need to discredit me also grew. I'd often hear comments that traveled back through the family to me. My anger and frustration became toxic. I believed if I spoke up at this point it would only seem like retaliation. He was buddies with police, doctors, and nurses. I was a single mom, divorced twice, with one ex in prison for drugs. Seriously, who would you believe? With God's love and biblical teachings on healing, forgiveness is a reality. Like Daddy used to say, "No problem has ever been solved with a hot head or a cold heart." I know this person is not happy, because secrets make you sick. My secrets made me terminal. After all, God won't heal what you don't reveal. He's had marital problems and, like most of us, thinks it's everyone else's fault. I have prayed for this person to be healed, to ask God's forgiveness, and be set free of his perversion and darkness.

As I write about family I'm reminded of a humorous, yet truthful, revelation God showed me about my character. Daddy used to say, "Character is what you are. Reputation is what people think you are." One day while praying, God gave me a funny analogy of who I'd actually been. There are so many people that are interested in doing genealogical searches on their families. Perhaps they are looking for things that explain certain career choices, or certain behaviors that may be inherited. It took me awhile, but I discovered that I was a descendent of the "Ate" family. I used to retaliate, intimidate, frustrate, hesitate, infuriate, manipulate, separate, aggravate, could not concentrate, was an ingrate, would not participate, failed to relate, thought I decided my fate, was always late, and of course, always chose to hate. I'm excited to say I have no more ties with this family. That bloodline has now been transfused with the precious blood of Jesus. You might criticize my "been through," but wait till you see my "break through!" God can change those who only want to *get* high, to only wanting to *serve* the most high.

Daddy passed away in 2004, and I've no doubt he's gone to be with the Lord. I'm equally happy that Mama calls Jesus her personal Savior. It's never too late to begin again.

As a result of all the anger I felt from the molestation in my early teens, keeping it buried so deep inside, I began to look for ways to anesthetize the hurt and pretend it didn't happen. This included drinking. I hung out with the wrong sort of kids, got in trouble, let my grades slip, and showed no interest in school. I skipped school, and eventually ran away from home. I would run away for a day or two, but my parents always brought me back. They always managed to find me, with the exception of the last time.

"Thanksgiving – When One Species Stops Gobbling and Another Begins"

Somewhere around the age of fifteen I became more defiant and my desire to test boundaries became more prevalent. Mama's family had been blessed with musical talent. I guess I inherited the musical gene from that side of the family. As a small child I would sing for our guests. My first solo performance was "Amazing Grace" at our church. I was only seven years old, but vividly remember the response of the congregation. I had no idea of the significance of that song. I never suspected what it would mean in my own life years later. "Amazing Grace" was written by a former slave ship captain named John Newton. Personally convicted of his actions and cruelty to others, Newton fought valiantly for the remainder of his life, with others, to see slavery abolished in the United Kingdom.

The pursuit of music was a constant dream. No surprise, I jumped at the opportunity to go to a major artist's concert with backstage passes. It's amazing the things we do for validation. While at the concert I met someone working on the tour. By the end of it I left with him. Little did I know this decision would start a horrible domino effect. When you're fifteen you believe in knights in shining armor, or in my case shiny buses, that whisk you away. While they might whisk you away, nothing guarantees they'll bring you back.

One night, in a drunken rage, I picked a fight with the new boyfriend. I woke up the next morning at the hotel, alone. The band and entire crew had left town. I had been left behind. I stupidly got out on the interstate and began to hitchhike. You've no idea how many times I have shuddered from what could have happened from that. I hitched a ride with a couple of "good old boy" truckers. They never put a foot wrong, but they lectured me constantly about the hazards of hitchhiking. I have to say it must have worked. I've never put my thumb out again. They were only going as far as Columbus, Georgia, so at that point they dropped me and my things at a little motel, handed me twenty dollars, and wished me good luck.

Since hitchhiking was no longer an option, I decided to get a job to earn enough money to get home. As good fortune would have it, this little motel needed another housekeeper. The housekeeping crew was a staff of two, with one spot available. The other benefit was room and board. There was a small mobile home owned by the motel. The other housekeeper lived there, and we agreed to be roommates and coworkers. It wasn't that bad, despite the trailer being a dump and the salary practically nonexistent. It felt good being independent, waking up, making my own breakfast, and getting to work on time. However, the novelty soon faded, and I began to really miss home.

There's no way I could have been serious about saving money. What my roommate and I didn't spend on food, we spent at the bar down the street. We'd play pool, sit at the bar and drink, go home and repeat it all over again the next night. May I remind you I was fifteen and why I was never carded boggles the mind. The heels were high and the mascara was perfect. But even a blind man could have seen I was a child. That is, until I met the blond haired, blue eyed boy I believed would make all my dreams come true. We shared the occasional glance before eventually speaking. This gradually evolved into playing pool, and later progressed into meeting up every night.

Back then we didn't have Karaoke. It was called Open Mike night. Every time I would sing he'd tell me how wonderful my voice was. I began to fall madly for this guy and believed he was falling for me. He'd tell me how beautiful I was and how he knew I could make it in the music business. He spoke of how affluent his family was and of their vast fortune. He assured me his mother could finance recording an album. This was everything a fifteen year old girl, who had no self-esteem, wanted to hear. When I told my roommate I was falling for him, I recall her saying "Niki, there's something about him I just don't trust." She was older, mid-twenties, and had seen a few of her own disasters. Here's the thing; when you're desperate for validation and someone is showering you with gifts and compliments, the natural thing to believe is she was jealous. Obviously. He wasn't lavishing attention her way. At some point he convinced me to go with him to Akron, Ohio to visit his mom for Thanksgiving. He talked me into quitting my job, packing all my things, and declared it was his job to

23

take care of me from that point on. The pattern was emerging. So, I packed, hugged my roommate goodbye, and started towards the nightmare.

As we wound our way through each State he began to say things like, "I don't like that outfit or that shirt on you, let's buy you something new." I never thought of it as controlling. In my mind he cared for me so much he wanted me to look good. Plus, I was getting all new things. I was hardly going to complain. We would go into shopping malls and department stores and he'd spend hundreds of dollars on clothes, boots, shoes, coats, until everything met with his approval.

On Thanksgiving Day, I noticed the more miles behind us, the more irritable he became. I assumed it was because we would be late for lunch. I didn't realize he was late for a deadline. By the time we reached Cincinnati he was driving like a mad man. 70 mph became 90 mph, 90 a 100 and so on. He began weaving in and out of cars so fast they went by in a blur. I have to be honest, I literally thanked God under my breath as the police lit us up and pulled us over. As we coasted to the side of the road he pulled out his ID, and threw his wallet in my lap stating, "Whatever you do, don't let them have this." The look on my face must have said it all, because he repeated it once more, this time through gritted teeth. Obediently, I hid it on me and sat quietly. As fast as his personality had changed saying this to me, it reverted back just as fast, as the officer approached the car. He politely explained we were late for Thanksgiving, but the officer insisted we needed to come with him.

We proceeded to the station, where he was told bail would have to be posted. Knowing he literally had thousands in his wallet, I began to reach in my purse. He glared at me in a way that stopped me dead in my tracks, and yet turned with a smile and replied, "I'll have to get my mom to wire it. I've lost my wallet." Shortly after that I went to the restroom, where curiosity got the better of me. Ok, I got the part about not wanting to pay a huge fine. But not enough to sit in a cell for six to seven hours when a flip of the wallet could have you back on your way in a minute. I remember feeling guilty for peeking at his personal things, which was soon replaced with confusion and fear. In the wallet were two IDs, both with his picture, each with a different name. What on earth was going on?

I've asked myself a million times why I didn't go straight out to the desk and show them what I'd found. I am now aware that by this time I had become conditioned, and had developed a twisted loyalty to this person. I was suffering from what is known as Stockholm syndrome. I believed he'd done so much for me, I couldn't betray him. If I'd only known. The biggest mistake we ever make in life is refusing to listen to wisdom from someone who has walked where we are headed. After hours and hours of waiting, he finally made bail. He was released. But I wasn't sure who I was leaving with.

"The Way To Happy Ever After - Don't Be *After* Too Much"

As we drove on to Akron, he became more and more agitated by my questions and inquiries of the IDs. This was the first, but certainly not last time, he backhanded me in the mouth and told me to never question him again. Reluctantly, he talked about stealing identities and cashing checks by the thousands. He had used a stolen machine that pressed or embossed the amounts to look like paychecks. He was constantly reiterating that he'd done all of this to take care of me. His dance with law enforcement had started long before me, but this is the abuser's nature. They always transfer blame and guilt to manipulate a situation. While I was certainly no choir girl, even in the midst of my juvenile delinquency, I knew how wrong all of this was, and would've never condoned such a fraudulent act. I may have had misguided bravery, but I certainly had no aspirations to reside in a 10x10 cell. There's nothing wrong with having nice things or receiving lovely gifts. We must be certain, however, there is not a price tag attached that may cost our soul. Like Daddy used to say, "Some people know the price of everything and the value of nothing." Judas bought a one way ticket to hell with thirty pieces of silver. What's buying your ticket? Is it pornography? Adultery? Addictions? Unforgiveness and hatred?

When we arrived in Akron, I walked in expecting a Norman Rockwell feast on the table. Mom was sitting at the table, but it was not with a turkey. There were two men sitting at the table with her and the first words out of her mouth were, "Is this it?" Not, "Is this her?" After the ordeal in the car, and feeling humiliated, all my hopes of her being my ally completely vanished. It was blatantly clear I was on my own. I declared I was leaving, not knowing where I was going, BUT I WAS LEAVING!!! I turned to walk out the kitchen door and was immediately grabbed around the waist by one of the men. I was dragged kicking and screaming upstairs to the third floor attic. I remember digging my fingernails into the wall, grabbing for the banister, and holding on as tight as possible. When I wouldn't let go, he would slam his fist on my knuckles till I released. I was thrown inside the dark room and, before I could scramble to my feet, the door was slammed and locked behind me.

It felt like hours that I kicked, screamed, and beat against the door trying to get out. It was only after I stopped, trying to compose my thoughts and figure a way out, that I realized I was not alone in the attic. There was a shaft of light coming through a very small opening, which must have been a window, but now boarded up. I heard a small voice from across the room say, "You'll never get out of here. No one will ever hear you." It was a young girl about my age and her brother. He was a couple years younger and deaf. The grip of fear paralyzed me, and I realized this was much more than a lover's argument. I knew something very dark was going on in this house, and I had just been pulled into the midst of it.

"Out Of One Abuse Comes Many"

I'm not sure how much time passed before I heard footsteps on the stairs. I knew someone was coming, and I immediately braced to fight my way out. Both of the men that had been downstairs came in and dragged me over to what was supposed to be a mattress, though it was less than an inch thick. I was shackled around the right ankle and told to shut up, or they would shut me up. They held me down and injected me for the first time with drugs. As I started to waft in and out, I could hear the girl across the room say, "If you just eat the food, they won't do this." I eventually passed out. When I woke I could tell something really bad had happened. I had been sexually assaulted but I didn't know by whom, or how many. This was the first of many times this occurred in this hell.

The conditions in the attic were deplorable. The stench was unbearable. What little food we received was, at best, barely edible. There were days they either neglected or forgot to bring food at all. No personal hygiene was allowed. We'd occasionally be taken down to the second floor for them to wash off food, feces or worse, when it became overwhelming to *them*. My abductor sexually assaulted me violently over the first few weeks, after which, he'd tell me what was expected of me. I would resist, refuse, and argue and then beg him to let me go. This ended with fierce beatings, each more violent than the last. I thought at one point I'd convinced him to let me leave. It had only convinced him to beat me worse. I eventually stopped asking, but resolved I would not stay there. Somehow, someway, I would get out.

The men, who were best described as vile, abused us without compassion. The more you cried and begged, the worse it was. Some were only there once. Others returned, but left little doubt of their intentions. I was being sexually assaulted every day. I became withdrawn and determined not to respond to the pain. My hatred fueled my constant thoughts of escape. Because I had not consented to any of my circumstances, this hatred later spilled over to anyone that delved into pornography or was considered promiscuous. It was years before I understood the concept of "invisible handcuffs". It's all force and coercion, just wrapped in different packages. I used to stand in judgment of women who traded their bodies for drugs, or danced in strip clubs. I am now aware that no one really wants to be exploited. We all just arrive there in different vehicles.

May I remind you, as previously stated, people that judge usually feel judged. I've often shared that I'm a redeemed serial killer. 1 John 3:15 says "Anyone who hates, abominates, detests his brother in Christ is at heart a murderer, and you know that no murderer has eternal life abiding persevering within him." I spent way too much time hating too many people, and where did it get me? Daddy used to say, "Unforgiveness is like drinking poison and then waiting for the other man to die." Proverbs 15:18 says, "A hot tempered man stirs up strife, but he who is slow to anger appeases contention." Daddy also said, "When you fly into a rage expect a rough landing."

God may allow you to live through things that you yourself may not have chosen, but he'll never ask you to live through more than his own son, Jesus. Can you imagine if Jesus would have refused to leave heaven, stomped his foot and said "Nope, I'm not doing it! They're gonna talk about me, they're gonna lie about me and oh, there's that cross thing. No, no, can't do it." What about Mary? What if she would have said, "Ok, I'll be the mother of Christ" but had a really bad attitude. What if she was constantly telling people to peel her grapes, while pointing at her belly and saying, "You do know who I am, right?" No. When she found out that she was going to deliver the Savior, she went to serve Elizabeth.

I remember one night catching a glimpse of what I thought was the moon. In actuality, it was probably only a street light. However, I wondered if my folks were looking at the same moon. Could they have given up on me by now, or did they believe I was dead? I recently spoke with my aunt, who remembers the night the police were at my house. My Mama was convinced that I'd run off with a boyfriend. But my Daddy was willing to do anything to find me and bring me home. We didn't have tools and systems available to bring children home like we do today. There was no internet. No Amber alerts. When we went missing our pictures ended up on milk cartons. Mine never made it that far. I have no doubt, had my Daddy known where I was, he would have walked all the way to Akron, if necessary, to bring me safely back home.

Aside from my fellow captives the only other person I had contact with who wasn't abusive was an extremely addicted young man named John. John did menial tasks in exchange for drugs. Although he was driven from one fix to the next there was something human about him. As time went on, his darting glances grew into small talk. Eventually I found a glimmer of hope, that he may not be too damaged to understand I needed his help. The first time I asked, he pondered less than a second before saying, "I can't do that, you know I can't do that!" When the retaliation didn't come, I knew he hadn't told on me and believed there was a chance. He was adamant he couldn't help. In fact, for a while, he stopped speaking to me at all. So imagine my shock one day, as he leaned in and whispered to me that he realized I didn't belong there and would be instrumental in getting me out. All those times before when I'd begged him to unlock the door and leave it open I would say, "They'll never know it was you." But he'd quickly shut me down. I could see the fear of these people in his eyes. He knew the type of people we were dealing with, and he didn't want to suffer at their hands the way we had. He didn't exactly get off scot-free. Many times I saw him get pushed, punched, slapped and hit on the head. He was constantly verbally abused.

Although he was a big boy, they kept the leash tight with the threat of withholding his drugs. The little bit of hope he'd given me was quickly dashed when I heard him adamantly proclaim to my abductor he had a great idea. He talked of taking me to a bar in downtown Akron to advertise. I can't tell you how devastated I was to have trusted him. Yet again, I'd been betrayed. He was persistent until my abductor finally agreed. On the scheduled night they brought me downstairs, put me in the shower, gave me some clothes and makeup and said, "Make yourself pretty." That was the last thing I wanted to be. Pretty had brought me a lot of unwanted attention.

"The Darker the Night, the Brighter the Light"

My abductor's mood was darker than usual that night. It was obvious he had been drinking, and most likely imbibing of the many products they sold. He kept saying he was tired of me, I didn't follow the rules, I was hard work, and more trouble than I was worth. He reminded me constantly of the consequences of disobeying him. The plan was to bring me into the bar, sit me on a stool, solicit some interest; then take me back to the van while John stood guard. As we sat down, John leaned over and while picking up an ashtray, whispered, "When I say run, get out the front door." I didn't trust anything he said by now, and wondered if he was trying to send me from one bad situation to worse. By now I had seen many twisted and inhumane things, so anything was possible.

As my abductor continued to drink he became more abusive, grabbing my hair and yanking my head back. Through gritted teeth, he would say things like "I should just slit your throat, throw you in the dumpster, or leave you out back in the alley. That's where you belong. That's all you're worth." He continued ranting that I was hard work, had cost him money and he didn't need the aggravation. I had no doubt to what he was referring. There was a particular incident in which one of the men who had viciously assaulted me had caused a great deal of pain. I was determined to remember every detail of his face. I swore if I ever escaped I'd find him and kill him. There was nothing rational in this thinking. But revenge is rarely, if ever, born from a rational point of view. All I knew was that I had an intense desire to see this man suffer, in the same way he had hurt me. As a result, he had complained to my abductor, and I received the worst beating I ever had the entire time I was there. He had beaten me on the head with a wooden clog (shoe) so hard, that I'd blacked out. It was morning when this took place, and when I woke up it was dark outside. I asked my fellow captive how many hours I'd been passed out. She replied, "Hours? You've been out for days. But business went on as usual." I still can't wrap my head around what kind of human being can sexually assault an unconscious fifteen year old girl.

I sat on the bar stool, compliant, in a room full of people. I was scared to say a word, but found myself scanning every face and every exit. My abductor's grip was so tight on my arm, the bruises left an intricate pattern of fingers. I asked him meekly if I could go to the bathroom. As I stepped off the stool his temper exploded. He again grabbed my hair, yanking my head back, while he pulled the knife from his pocket and repeated his plan of slitting my throat and throwing me out. His inebriation outweighed his logic, and he began to make a scene as he dragged me towards the hallway leading out back.

I felt the blade on my neck and began to try and reason with him that he'd only imagined my lack of compliance. I would have told him anything to stay alive. Drunk and unsteady on his feet, he continued dragging me down the hallway to the exit in back where the van was parked. I knew if we ever got past the back door, it was over. Just as we crossed the threshold, two prostitutes, who had been working the room, came out of the bathroom. For a moment he forgot about me as he began threatening them. One of the girls, and a couple of guys, began wrestling him for the knife. I ran outside, not thinking about which direction, but ended up out front as John had suggested. I was barely out the door, when a truck door opened and I heard a young man's voice ask, "Are you Niki? I'm Buster, come on, get in."

I stood there on the street, my shirt ripped and blood running down my neck, until his girlfriend stepped out and guided me over to the truck. As Buster drove through the night his girlfriend used the stack of White Castle napkins from the dashboard to clean the blood from my neck and chin. We were headed to his friend's house. Buster's friend Chrissie and her family had little in worldly or monetary goods, but what they had they willingly shared with me. It was many years later, when Chrissie and I talked again, that she revealed what happened as I sat in the truck when Buster went inside. When he proposed I stay with them the entire family adamantly refused with the exception of Chrissie, who was also my age. Once Buster shared what would likely happen were I not to stay, Chrissie fought valiantly for my life, although we'd never met. There are just some people in this world who are born to be heroes. She is mine. They had no extra money and I began to feel like a burden, but shame and trauma kept me from calling my family for help. Buster came by occasionally to try to give us updates. One day he said the police were looking for my abductor for ID theft, fraud, and counterfeiting. I also learned they were looking to question him about a disappearance of another young woman from Georgia, where he'd met me.

I eventually called my parents, and we were reunited. The abuse and trauma left with me with many issues that would continue to cloud my judgment and affect my thinking for many years to come. I'd love to say that was the darkest moment of my life. "But the devil don't quit that easy." If he fails with one attempt, he will better equip the next one.

"Ignorance Is Bliss"

Romans 12:2 says "And be not conformed to this world: but be ye transformed by the renewing of your mind, that ye may prove what is that good, and acceptable and perfect will of God." In other words, Jesus saved my soul. It was up to me to change the "stinkin thinkin." When I later became a Christian I didn't immediately develop amnesia. I still remembered how to behave badly. I still remembered the things that caused me pain. I was still as unbalanced as I'd been the day before I became a Christian. Your attitude is just that, your attitude! It's up to you to change it, no one else. Daddy used to say, "If there are things in your life you don't like, change them. If you can't change them, change the way you think about them." I look back now and realize I was the one responsible for how long I remained miserable. People would try to tell me that I was difficult, angry and that I had issues. I believed it was everyone *but* me. Ignorance is bliss.

To date, we've only had one president who was also a pastor: President Garfield. Like Daddy, Garfield was responsible for some pretty amazing quotes, like "I am a poor hater." As you can see, haters have been around a lot longer than reality TV. President Garfield was shot, but not immediately killed, and left to suffer in horrible summer heat. It was so bad, the military developed a prototype of air conditioning by blowing fans over blocks of ice. It's reported to have lowered the temperature in the room by as much as eleven degrees. Although Joseph Lister had taught antiseptic measures more than a decade earlier, a very stubborn doctor by the name of W.D. Bliss prodded and poked with unwashed, dirty hands trying to locate the bullet. In truth, the wound was not fatal. The stubborn ignorance of Dr. Bliss, who refused to change his methods, is what killed President Garfield. So you see, ignorance really is "Bliss."

We cannot continue with old, dirty, stubborn behavior and expect different results. In fact, that is the very definition of insanity. When I finally invited Jesus to live in my heart, it required decades of eviction notices for anger, pride, shame and selfishness. They all had to leave, making room enough for Jesus to live comfortably in my heart. God gives us feelings and emotions to control, not the other way around. I often tell ladies, we are responsible for the way we treat other people, not the way they treat us.

With PTSD (Post Traumatic Stress Disorder) you often relive the experiences that traumatized you. There are nightmares and triggers that either take you right back or send you spiraling out of control. We are often out of control, trying to be "in control." If I'm honest, I became a Christian, as I will later explain, with a selfish motive. It's true. I got saved simply because I did not want to go to hell. Daddy used to say, "Some people get saved to get good fire insurance." I guess I was one of them. When we are saved it should be the beginning of a lifelong process of change. Otherwise, we become a bit like Peter. At one point in his life he became whatever crowd he was in.

In Matthew 28, Jesus says "Come to me, all who are weary and heavy laden. Take my yoke upon you because I am humble and gentle and you will find rest for your souls." In other words, we don't need to pour our hearts out on Facebook. We go to God's book for our answers. It's never too late for redemption; ask the guy who was hanging next to Jesus. You may think God is mad at you. Perhaps you've yelled at him, demanding answers. Well, guess what, he can take it. He doesn't operate the way man does. He doesn't let a thought or a deed you've done get stuck in his head. He's always rooting for you to make it. To guide you, love you, and lead you. The enemy hates someone who is determined, but he is terrified of a comeback kid. He knows they will come back at everything he hurls at them, with God by their side. King David was a comeback kid. His father voted him the least likely to succeed, and yet he slayed Goliath. He was the apple of God's eye, and he still allowed lust to cloud his mind with some really bad decisions. Peeping Tom and murderer. Does that sound like a King? And yet, although there were consequences, he was still forgiven.

If you are reading this in jail or prison, you must deal with the consequences of your actions. But it doesn't stop you from having forgiveness. It doesn't have to define who you *can* be. It doesn't matter your background, your education, or your mistakes. God uses everyone and everything, from cowboy boots to business suits. Never give up! You can't *lose* hope, but you can surely give it away. Maybe you've been mistreated by family. I know what it's like to be lied about by my own family. In fact, there are some family members that would probably rather hug a barrel cactus than hug me. And there's a few that I could say the same about. Don't let that sway you. Isaiah 54:17 says, "No weapon that has been formed against you shall prosper and every tongue that will rise against you in judgment shall be shown to be in the wrong." We've all made mistakes, even the disciples. They weren't perfect. When they weren't acting like the dirty dozen, they were twelve angry men. They watched Jesus daily, and they still struggled with bad behavior. Sometimes we encounter things that require us to stretch out of our comfort zones.

A perfect example is in Luke 5, where Jesus encountered a frustrated and worn out Peter. He'd been fishing all night, hadn't caught a thing, which meant no money. You can imagine how he must have rolled his eyes when Jesus said to launch deeper. He even argued back, reminding him how they'd been up all night and caught nothing. Like Jesus didn't know. How often do we try to remind God of things, because they haven't happened yet? However, Peter did say, "Nevertheless at thy word" or because you said so Lord, we're going to do this again. The next time out, it took two boats to hold all the fish. The nets were breaking and the boats were about to sink. How many times are we only one push away from a miracle and give up? Daddy used to say, "Even a mosquito knows you have to go to work to get a slap on the back." There is power in positive. No one wants to hang out with defeated, grumpy, miserable people. Miserable people want you to ask how they're doing, so they can tell you. I have compassion, but I have learned to keep the boundaries healthy. In other words, sometimes you might have to throw a few Jonahs off the boat to get peace. It's all too easy to play the hard card. "It's too hard."

In both the old and new testaments the word speaks about separating sheep from goats. I always used to wonder why. Then one day it dawned on me. Sheep follow the master, goats like to butt. "But you don't know how hard I've had it." "But you don't know my circumstances." "But you don't know my husband." "But you don't know my wife." It's time we stopped dragging those "buts" around. Pick them up, and declare that Jesus did not come for us to remain in the bondage of the "buts". Stop living in denial. We've all heard what denial stands for, right? *Don't Even kNow I Am Lying.*

When I look back, I believe the dominating emotions that ruled my life far too long, were anger, guilt, and shame. Anger, for all that had been done to me that I didn't ask for. Guilt, because I felt that in some way I caused it to happen. And shame, because it was unbearable to think anyone could know the horrors that had been done to me. As if it were my fault. Isn't it strange when something attacks our bodies, like a car accident or an illness, we know it's our responsibility to seek medical help? We don't ask for bad things to happen. Terrible infections and diseases attack even health conscious people, all day long. It's nothing they've brought on, but it still needs to be dealt with. So why is it when we are hurt or wounded by other people or situations, we manage to think it's everyone else's problem to fix? Why don't we reach for that spiritual mental wellness, as quickly as we do the physical?

We have become the Band-Aid generation. Hating, hurting, and blaming those that have inflicted pain. Anger will never make it go away or keep it from happening. But that pain *will* keep you from the destiny God has called you for. Healing comes only after we identify the hurt. Once we identify the core root problem, then we can get busy doing what's needed to get healthy, especially applying God's word and walking it out. It takes work, perseverance, effort, faith, and patience: All the things a microwave generation doesn't want to hear. I've lived a lot of my life in denial. It's like tying a piece of string around your wrist. Once, you can break it with little or no effort. Twice, it's a little harder, but doable. Three, it cuts into the skin and can't be done without pain. Every time you wrap denial around who and where you are in life, it becomes harder and harder to break out of it. Daddy used to say "A good soldier is always fighting or he's learning how to." In 2 Timothy 2:3, it says, "Take with me your share of the hardships and suffering which you are called to endure as a good first class soldier of Christ Jesus."

The problem is we tend to get lazy. We want God, or someone else, to do the work for us. We pray selfish prayers, giving God a wish list or a hit list. There *is* such a thing as a stupid prayer. Something I read on a key chain that was meant to be a laugh, unfortunately, is the way a lot of us pray. It said, "Lord if you can't make me skinny, please make all my friends fat." You may laugh, as I did, until I honestly acknowledged we've all prayed something similar, if not those exact words. Anything worth having will require both time and hard work. It doesn't come in a shot, a pill, or a drink. If you sit around doing nothing, waiting for your ship to come in, you might find it's called hardship.

When Jesus said, "Ye shall know the truth and the truth shall set you free," it was an action. You can know about losing weight all day, but if you don't make it an action, you stay unhealthy. You can know how to overcome an addiction, but if you don't put the effort in, you stay addicted. Some people are like blisters; they only show up when the hard work is done. Life has no shortcuts, and no one can do it for you. I know it's hard to shout when somebody's stepping on your toes, but like Daddy used to say, "If someone is giving you good, Godly advice that can change your life and it rubs your fur the wrong way, it might be time to turn the cat around."

"It's Better to Give All Your Heart Than A Piece of Your Mind"

Sadly, these days, too many of us have had failed marriages. I failed not once, but twice. Of course, over the years, I always told it with the bad light falling on my ex-husbands. When you get honest, you begin to notice every time you point a finger at someone else's mistakes there's three fingers pointing back at you. My first husband and I were terribly young. Far too young for marriage or the responsibility of parenthood. It was a short marriage, producing our only daughter. I used to get terribly upset at how irresponsible and absent he was in our daughter's life. When it wasn't parties, it was incarcerations. We divorced shortly after he was first sentenced to prison. He would be incarcerated on and off for years, struggling with his addictions right up until his death. Shortly before he died, I am told he came to know the Lord and was working on putting the pieces of his life back together. I hope this to be true.

My second husband also struggled with his demons. Alcohol and drugs pulled at his soul for years. He did step up to the plate, however, as a father figure for my daughter. Although she saw ugly fights and harsh exchanges, there was never a question he had true affection and love for her. I am told that he wrestled with the loss of her in his life after we divorced. She still communicates with him frequently. He's now clean and in church, and God has blessed him with a Godly wife who is not only beautiful on the outside, but inside as well.

It's so easy to blame mistakes on everyone else. But that robs you of the ability to heal and grow. Yes, there were some ugly things during those marriages that were said and done to me. But I was far from perfect. My daughter's father may have missed a lot of her life, but he wasn't the only one to drop the ball. Although she never endured physical abuse, there were other ways my behavior impacted her negatively. Until she was around three, how often did my parents take her for a night, which turned into a week or more? My youth, and feelings of inadequacy, often overwhelmed me. At least with them, I reasoned, she was physically safe. However, as a result, there were bonding issues we work on even now. We forget how important listening really is. We *all* want to be heard. Even children. How many times do we say I'll never treat my children the way I was, and yet slip right into that same slot? She'd want to tell me something exciting, and I would shush her while on the phone or watching TV. I'd come in from work and want to be left alone, or often ended up criticizing her instead of praising. I was turning into my mother. Let's be honest, we all say stupid things as parents. Such as "Look at me, I'm talking to you,-"Don't look at me like that!" Or "You better stop that crying or I'll give you something to cry about." It's no wonder kids get confused. Sometimes we don't talk enough about what we *should* to our kids, and often too much of what we *shouldn't*.

God has taught me how to take responsibility for my actions that helped to end these marriages. I've no doubt these marriages were not meant to be. But the Holy Spirit has reminded me how quick I was to judge their addictions and short comings. I'd enable their addictions, by going with them to bars and parties, and then complain when situations got out of hand. They were addicts; what did I expect? What may have happened if instead I had treated them with Godly, unconditional love? Until you understand addiction, you tend to be a little pious and self-righteous about it, whether you admit it or not. Instead of hunting them down when they were at bars, or hitting them with the machine gun mouth of criticism once they walked through the door, I should have been praying for them. They would both eventually return home, knowing I'd be gunning for bear. They were usually in battle mode, full of guilt, coming in the door. How much would God's love have disarmed and diffused many volatile situations? After all, love gives the advantage, it doesn't take advantage. We look for other people's faults with the enthusiasm of digging for gold. We should treat our friends like family, and our family like friends. I'm reminded of a couple things that Daddy would say like "A pinch of don't say it, is worth a pound of didn't mean it." Or "The best revenge is the one not taken." Most of the time, things said in anger are never worth the damage caused. On a funny note, the only one that usually ever hears both sides of an argument is the next door neighbor. Be careful condemning those who miss the mark. God has a way of letting you get a taste of what you think you're superior to. He allows us to be knocked off our high and mighty perches. It's up to us to learn lessons from it.

After my second marriage ended and a short time working in the medical field, I gave up my halfhearted attempt at nursing and moved a step closer to my first love, music. I suppose the brief time I pursued nursing was my way of admitting I needed healing. Perhaps if I was involved in caring for someone else, it would in some way make me better. We cannot be effective in other's lives if we have not identified and addressed our own issues. When this doesn't happen, we jump from job to job, marriage to marriage, and church to church.

I took courses at the local community college for broadcasting and was hired straight into a local station as on-air talent. You may recall, I had been singing for my family and church since childhood, and had read somewhere many well-known singers were once deejays. I figured if it worked for them, why not me? You have no idea how many frustrated performers there are in broadcasting, theatre, or TV. They will settle for work as roadies or crew just to be near it. I had been in and out of bands from around thirteen and wrote my first song at ten. I was frequently in recording studios, singing for others, or recording my own original music.

One of my daughter's earliest memories, is sitting by my feet in a sound booth when she was four or five years old. She sat perfectly still, and everyone was amazed how well she understood, at such a young age.

After transitioning from small market radio to a larger medium, the opportunity to meet music people came with the territory. One night, while performing in a club after a celebrity golf tournament, I was approached by a producer/writer named Jack from Nashville. He stood by the front door, and sent word asking if I'd come speak with him for a moment. The gist of the conversation is that he saw potential and strongly urged me to come to Nashville. When I invited him into the club to have a seat and continue talking, he said," I'm only here to pick up Paul from the golf tournament." (I don't feel it's my place to give Paul's full name. Especially in lieu of how inebriated he was that night). Jack answered me by saying, "Clubs aren't my thing. I'm a Christian. I'm only here to bring him back to the hotel." He gave me his card and suggested I put together a two song demo, and, if interested, get back with him. Excited, but leery, I stuck his business card in my jeans pocket and returned to the crowded, noisy club.

"Echoes Are Accurate but Tell You Nothing New"

During the next few weeks, I began to make calls and inquiries to various studios and agencies in Nashville about this man's claims and character. There were no internet searches back then, but all who knew him had nothing but good to say. As a result of these calls, I struck up a friendship with someone at a prominent management company named Chico. Apparently there were a lot of "David's" around, and the story goes while on tour with Willie Nelson, he was given the nickname "Chico", and it stuck. Chico was a no nonsense, Vietnam vet. He spoke music fluently, and was very clear he didn't have time for anyone who wasn't serious. He also assured me that once in Nashville, he would help me avoid the beaten path. I don't honestly remember who suggested the studio I recorded my demos to send to Nashville, but there's no doubt God had a plan.

Of all the studios in North Carolina, I ended up in a home studio of a man named Milton Smith. It turns out he'd played professionally with some great country artists. It was rumored he was actually hired to play for Elvis before his death. The one thing I do know for certain is that he played many years for Tammy Wynette. After I settled in Nashville, I had many conversations with some of Tammy's people. Their admiration and respect for Milton was undeniable. He did a fabulous job producing, playing on my demo, and singing back-up vocals. The biggest impact that Milton had on me was his testimony of walking away from it all to serve God, his family, and church.

This was unlike anything I could wrap my head around. Here he was at the top of the ladder, where we're all clamoring to be, and he just let go. He walked away, back to anonymity and routine. Milton witnessed to me that day, using scripture, what does it profit a man to gain the world but lose his soul? He told me how Jesus would have done everything, even died, if I'd been the only one. This would not be the last time I heard these words.

I eventually went to Nashville, and moved in with Jack and his wife. I learned early on if anyone asked what brought me to Nashville, to always say, I-40. There is a saying, "Nashville eat their young". This town, like many others, always has someone waiting to pounce and exploit the naïve. I began doing backup vocals in studios and shows. I was fortunate to witness the hustle and bustle backstage at the Opry. I remember meeting Bill Monroe, Ricky Skaggs, and the ever flamboyant showman, Porter Wagner, all in one night. I remember excitedly calling home to tell friends about going to Leon Russell's house in Gallatin, Tennessee, and meeting songwriter Marc Beeson as he showcased the now famous song by Restless Heart, "When She Cries." Jack and his wife were also giving me some intros of their own, to a guy named Jesus.

Being Christians, they made sure to take every opportunity to witness. I remember walking in the kitchen finding his wife reading her bible and feeling so agitated I wanted to scream. I was so annoyed when they invited me to church, saying, "We want you to meet Barbara Mandrell's piano player. He goes to our church". I couldn't get away from it, no matter how hard I refused. I now know that it's called conviction. When I blatantly refused to attend church, Jack's wife ever so discreetly started leaving little cassettes on my nightstand. I knew what they were. It was recordings of a preacher from Oklahoma named Billy Joe Daugherty. I was determined not to listen, and yet one night I did. I heard him preach a sermon how Jesus came to this earth, walked and healed, and if I'd been the only one, he would have done it just for me. The same thing Milton had told me. Years later, I would write a song about that sermon called *Greatest Story*. I'd love to say at this point I surrendered all and gave my heart to the Lord but just the opposite; I became angrier than ever.

As I moved deeper in the Nashville circle, I also became more disenchanted. We act as though when we encourage or praise someone, it somehow takes away from who we are when in fact, the more you praise others, the more you grow and feel better about yourself. Most of all, it pleases God, and there is no approval more worthy. How often did I come face to face with some of the greatest musicians and entertainers in the world, but let my own insecurities rob that moment because of jealousy, and feeling I didn't measure up?

I would love to say this only happens in the secular world, but in fact, I have seen it alive and well in churches. When these emotions are left unchecked, mainly jealously, you can't appreciate or enjoy the blessings that God has placed around you. You are so consumed with what everyone is thinking of you, good or bad. It took a long time for me to figure out that God wasn't as impressed with my ability as he was with my availability. We have a hard time praising other people's promotions, as though it were a one size fits all. We get far too caught up in what *we* think we're supposed to be, instead of what God wants us to be. I'll give you an example. When I first became a Christian, I automatically assumed because of my background in music, I was called to be a Christian recording artist, or worship leader in a huge church. I didn't need to be a worship leader, simply one of the lead worshipers. Looking back, if I had listened closely when God first whispered ministry in my ear, I would have heard, "But it will take you about twenty years to be ready for what I'm sending your way." We get impatient and spoiled, when we don't get things *when we think* we're supposed to have them. Why do you think so many people move from church to church? They expect the pastor to be responsible for their spiritual maturity, as though they should have no part in the work. It's like sending a child to Kindergarten, then moving them to another school. Guess what? They are still in Kindergarten. If you are in a church and have not grown, moving to another church will not make you a scholar. Incidentally, we get easily offended at church and often leave. Isn't it ironic that when drug dealers, abusive spouses, or bartenders treat us badly, we continue to go back for more?

When we have low self-esteem and something appears to be going right, we will always sabotage it to feel in control. There is a difference between arrogance and confidence. When we are arrogant, we try to convince everyone to believe things about ourselves. The hardest sell is "ourselves". When we are confident, we don't care what others believe. No matter what others think, we are comfortable in the skin God gave us. Another one of Daddy's brilliant stories comes to mind. An older lady was exiting a general store as a young man entered. She batted her eyes in a coyish way and said, "Why thank you", even though he hadn't uttered a word. The store owner smiled knowingly at the young man as he questioned the encounter. "Why did she say thank you?" the young man asked. "Because", the store owner replied, "the battery in her hearing aid was whistling, and she thought it was you." Now I don't condone wolf whistles, but this shows how this woman's confidence gave her the ability to see herself in a positive light. Her age didn't define her, nor her hearing loss.

I know the conviction to change my life was beginning to take hold. I did what I'd always done before, ran. Of course, I used the excuse I needed a change from Nashville, but that was so far from true. We always want people to see the image that presents us in the best light; no matter how false. It reminds me of another story Daddy once told of a farmer driving down the road and spotting painted targets on his neighbor's barn. Upon closer inspection, he saw that each target had been shot dead center of the bull's-eye. He'd known his neighbor for over twenty years and knew he was no marksman. Upon questioning his friend, it was revealed that he had indeed painted the targets. When the farmer asked who did the shooting, he was shocked to hear the neighbor reply, "I did." He then asked how he'd managed to hit with such accuracy, to which the neighbor replied, "I just shot up the barn and then painted the targets around it." Isn't that what we do? We shoot randomly and wildly into the barn and then paint what we want people to see.

Three years old and the music bug had bitten. I couldn't play this, then massive, guitar, but it didn't stop me dragging it everywhere and strumming wildly. My poor family!

Around the time I ran away. Body language says it all. Arms folded and mad at the world. If only my parents could have heard the noise in my head.

Holding my baby daughter as my Daddy looks on. His look said it all. He knew how much I loved her, but also how much I feared I would fail her.

My daughter right before spray mode.
I know it's before ......because you can see her, not fog!

Trying to climb the music ladder. Every step is slippery,
especially when you're barely holding on.

The only place I ever felt comfortable was behind a microphone. Once the music stopped the memories returned loud and clear.

Daddy as a young man. He always had a smile for everyone.

Daddy in the tobacco field. He worked hard, but never complained.

The mischievous look in Daddy's eye, right before he shared one of his humorous nuggets of wisdom. Taken only a few months before he left this world.

The day I married my best friend and true love. I've
never trusted another man, besides my Daddy, more.

"Bananas Don't Get Skinned, Until They Leave the Bunch"

After leaving Nashville, I returned to North Carolina. I moved into government housing in a less than desirable neighborhood, dependent on government assistance. I walked away from a promising career in a prominent neighborhood in Hendersonville, Tennessee. I traded a home on a lake, for the hood and government cheese. Some people will do anything to run from God, huh? I knew this couldn't be a permanent solution, and began to search for jobs. On one of the many sleepless nights, channel surfing, I came upon one of the Christian networks. That evening, Jeff Fenholt, former rocker and Broadway star of Jesus Christ Superstar, shared his testimony. I don't know Jeff personally, but I can tell you God used every word he spoke to reach into my heart. He spoke of the need to be validated, wanting fame, only to find he was emptier than before. All of the things Milton, Jack, and his wife had tried to tell me in Nashville came flooding back. I knelt alone beside my sofa, and for the first time in my life, had a real conversation with God. I was very honest with him that I'd never gotten it right before. I'd believed myself saved before, but this time he was definitely driving. I couldn't do it my way anymore. I began reading my bible, praying, and attending church. In a short amount of time, I found a job with a local orthopedist. This provided the finances to move to a better neighborhood and eventually buy a car.

Within a couple of years, my daughter and I moved to Greenville, South Carolina. I began to work for HIS radio, a Christian contemporary station, as an announcer. I began to feel God giving me glimpses of what he wanted me to do in ministry. However, sometimes it's supposed to be a glimpse and we think it's right now. I began a music ministry called "Out of the Fire" and I would sing, speak and give my testimony at women's groups, churches, events, and women's prisons. I really wanted to help make a difference in other women's lives, but the ministry always struggled financially.

To put it bluntly, my daughter and I were living paycheck to paycheck, and donation to donation. I look back now and see a lot of lessons learned from that time. One of the hardest lessons came when we found ourselves with nothing left and facing eviction. How could God do this to me? I now see he did it *for* me. Our best guidance comes when we stop questioning every single thing that we are asked to do. We can't pray God, use me, use me, use me, and then complain we feel used.

As I've said many times before, manipulation does not want guidance, it wants agreement. I often tell the ladies I work with, "If you can't take correction, don't expect direction." In fact, manipulation or lying to get a result, or something you want, is considered the same as witchcraft in the eyes of God. In John 21:18 he tells us when we are young and immature, we go where we want, answering to no one. When we are older and more mature, we are girded or belted, so that we can be led where we need to go. We want that correction, to get his direction. God will let you, as we say in the south, run buck wild. But when you are tired of running on empty or into brick walls, you cannot imagine the freedom of not having to figure it out. How easy it is to hand the belt or reins to God and say "Lead me. I'm so tired of trying to figure this out." God's GPS. Translated - God's Perfect Solution. He doesn't only know the way. He *is* the way. Saved, but stubborn, I was still trying to push against everything God was trying to teach me. I wasn't ashamed of music, but I struggled hard to keep my abuse silent. It's funny how we assume what God wants. But it's amazing when we let him have the reins and see what he can do. He can turn our trash to treasure. I used to feel like trash, but God says I'm recycled.

After the eviction, it seemed the right choice was to return to North Carolina to be near family. The last speaking engagement in Greenville, SC was for a large women's group. That night I received more love offerings than the entire time I'd been speaking. It was the amount I needed, right to the penny, to pay for a moving truck, deposit, first month's rent, and utilities to be turned on in North Carolina. It also covered the gas and food for the trip, right to the penny. You see, God told Sarah and Abraham that he would bless them with a child. But like me, Sarah got tired of waiting, and she had Abraham lie down with Hagar, their maid or bond woman. Ishmael was born. God was very clear. He didn't need help with his promises. Much later, he kept his word and gave Abraham and Sarah a son, Isaac. I realize now I started with an Ishmael ministry, but God was bringing me the Isaac ministry for the finale.

I can't help but be reminded of a group of young people to which I shared the Abraham/Sarah story with years ago. One particular young man didn't seem especially interested, until I mentioned Hagar, the bond woman. Sensing a shift in his attention, I was curious what had been the breakthrough moment that had him so captivated. Imagine my surprise to find out that he hadn't had a spiritual awakening, but a hormonal one. You see, he assumed that bond woman referred to a James Bond woman. Only in the imagination of youth could someone logically place tuxedoes and sports cars alongside tents and camels.

If God has called you for something, it will happen when he knows you are prepared for the job. I'm not saying you won't have struggles, but you don't need to pound on doors that aren't ready to open. Things may feel difficult as you wait. We've all heard that as God closes one door, he opens another. Daddy used to say, "That's true, but he didn't promise we wouldn't have some hell in the hallway." The word tells us that we are to be faithful in the little things, before God can trust us with the big things. Or again, as Daddy used to say, "Big doors swing on little hinges." How do you behave when you think no one is watching? Do you hold the elevator for someone who is twenty feet away? Or pretend you don't see them because you're late for an appointment? You might think no one is watching, but God is. He's far more interested in how you behave in private, than how you behave in public. You can't have a real public relationship with God before first having a real private one. I've heard so many people make the argument, "but everyone else acts this way." The bible tells us we are to be different; that we are to be in this world, but not of this world. In essence, aliens. I don't know about you, but this E.T. is planning on going home.

"Money Don't Buy Love -But It Keeps the Kids Calling"

Rocky Mount had no Christian radio stations in the area at the time I returned. So I took a job as a morning show host at a country station. I worked the early on-air shift, and afterwards, spent a good deal of time doing production, writing voiceovers, and producing commercials. This was the introduction of clients hearing my voice, and as I moved from station to station, the demand supported my new vocation of doing full time voiceovers. But that's jumping ahead.

By this time, I'd been a single mom for years. My daughter was becoming a teenager, and I began to question who this child was. I recognized the face, but there was very little else familiar. Her attitude, personality, dress, and even friends, took dramatic turns. The lack of a positive male, with the exception of my aging father, began to take its toll. I watched and argued as she went from one disastrous boyfriend to the next. Watching me migrate from one abusive relationship to another didn't exactly lay the best groundwork for a good example. Her anger and hormones, along with my frustration, grew to a toxic level to say the least.

As a parent, I can tell you I have failed, bailed, and run off the rails more times than I care to admit. Here I was, supposed to be this Godly woman, and yet we'd have screaming matches all the way to church. I can't tell you how many times I ducked from remotes and phones being thrown at my head. I screamed as loud as she did, sometimes louder. There were numerous times we would be driving down the road, her in the back seat mouthing off, me swerving all over, trying to swat her, and people behind us probably thinking, "There's Jesus stickers on the bumper, and crosses hanging in the rear view mirror. That car must be stolen".

We did not behave like Christians should behave. Neither of us. I, however, will take the brunt of that. After all, I was the parent. Yes, she was a teenager and should have respected me. But I had missed the opportunity to lay that moral foundation all those many years ago.

I say this with conviction. We have to start the minute our children are born, teaching them the things that God wants them to know. The word says train them up in the way they should go, and they'll not depart from it. It's never too late to start, however. My daughter has the very same tools that I have. To forgive, to grow, and to know God. It now becomes her choice whether or not she uses them.

One of the biggest arguments my daughter and I often had on Sunday mornings was that she was always late. She had an obsession with hair spray. I'd walk in her room and literally couldn't see for the fog of hair spray. As soon as you made contact, the brain cells began to ping. You can only imagine when her friends came for sleepovers what it was like. All of them donning their personal can of spray. Incidentally, why do they call it sleepovers, when they do anything but? If a storm would have hit our house and everything else blown away, she still wouldn't have had a hair out of place. We might have traveled more, if we hadn't had to take the fifty gallons of Aqua Net. I'm just kidding. It was only ten.

Always speak to your child in love, whether in conversation or discipline. It must always be balanced, and never in anger. We must teach our children that discipline and submission to authority is vital in a healthy life. If we don't teach our children to submit to authority, they will at some point in their life have no choice but to submit, whether it be to a judge, or eventually God.

We should also teach our children Exodus 20:12. "To honor thy father and thy mother that the days be long upon the land which the Lord thy God giveth thee." It doesn't say, unless they treat you bad and don't give you everything you ever wanted. Then you can be nice and only call them on a holiday, or if you need something, or if you're bored and have no one else to talk to. No, it doesn't say that. This is the only commandment with a promise attached to it.

Read the Ten Commandments for yourself. What does honor mean? It means to speak well of them, and to act in a way that shows courtesy and respect. Parents have a special place in the sight of God. All parents! But especially Godly ones. I know I keep emphasizing how important balance is. This is another area: Our parents. We either hold our parents emotionally hostage for every mistake they've ever made, or we elevate them to this unrealistic pedestal we can never live up to. We have to remember, they are human and they've had dreams, goals, and disappointments just like us. You don't have to agree with how they think, or how they live. You do, however, need to respect them. I've often said, we don't have to see eye to eye, to love heart to heart.

Picking up where I left off, regarding my new job, it was at this time, the radio station owner decided to upgrade the signal on the tower and called in a tower crew. I remember meeting the owner of the company, thinking how arrogant and obnoxiously rude he was. A week or so passed, and he began to try to make conversation with me. I'd politely respond and then head back to the control room, production room, or my office.

Prior to digital, on-air personalities had to do meter readings before each shift. I had stepped back into the engineering area to do so, and saw I had company. The owner of the tower company began to make small talk, and eventually asked me out. I don't remember what excuse I gave, but did so politely and bolted. The next day one of the girls at the station charged into my office and asked," Are you crazy? This man's a pilot. He owns his own company and he's richer then Elvis." (Well, that wasn't exactly true.) She continued on, "And you said no"? A friend at my church and I spoke at length about this. Everything in my discernment told me this was not a good idea. But my friend assured me I was just afraid of commitment and needed to take a chance. My grandma's words came back to me that it's better to be a poor man's darlin' than a rich man's slave. Why do we never listen? My radar had been accurate, but I was willing to listen to people, more than the Holy Spirit, because it suited my wants. A prime example of why we cannot cherry pick what we *do* and *do not do*, in God's word. I was the woman who my friends, when seeking advice about dating men, would jokingly remark, not to go out A.N.A (Against Niki's Advice). Like I actually had a clue. I think I used to view God, for a long time, as just another man to dominate me. God would heal that broken perspective. But not before I found myself in another dysfunctional setting.

I began to wear down from the weight of finances, single parenting and, quite frankly, trusting needs more than trusting God. I began what I believed was a cautious relationship with this man. I had become financially overwhelmed, and felt like I was about to lose everything. The thought of having a mate to carry this burden was more than a little tempting. Too often, women pray for God to bring them a Boaz, but get impatient and settle for a Bozo. As far as the financial, Daddy used to say, "They can't get blood out of a turnip but they sure can repossess them." I wasn't anxious to have my turnips repossessed, and so it began. In the beginning he would mention that he'd seen my bible in the car and talked about going to Bible College. As time passed and defenses dropped, things began to change. From former experiences with my abductor, you would think I'd have stuck to my guns. I'm sorry to say patterns don't change that easily. I not only became involved with this man, but entered into an immoral relationship out of marriage. When you step out of God's law, you invite a whole lot of evil into your house. Daddy always taught me, "A lesson learned hard is a lesson well learned." I knew the consequences of my actions were inevitable, but I never imagined how far they would take me. I won't list every detail of this two year relationship, but physical and mental abuse took place. Again, I allowed myself to be totally dependent on someone who wanted to control me. Everything came from him. He would buy expensive jewelry and gifts, and if I didn't behave the way he thought I should, he'd take it back until I was good again. By this time, he had isolated me enough that I began to lose contact with my church. Quite frankly, I became angry at both the church and God. Just like so many others, I walked into this but blamed everyone else for it. I asked God to deliver me from temptation but left a forwarding address.

After a couple of years in this relationship, I began to try and devise a way out. When he was generous, he would hand me money, gifts, etc. But his personality would go from happy to violent like a flash. Little by little, I began to hide some money in a sock. As fights grew more violent, so did the infidelity. I would be sitting in the office talking with him, as he sat on the other side of the desk, chatting and making dates with women in towns where he had upcoming jobs.

Don't misunderstand. I was allowed to go out on my own, leave to shop, etc. So you may ask, why didn't you leave before you did?

Unless you have been in a situation where over time you are slowly convinced that you're worthless, you can't understand. You stay, although it's unhealthy and unsafe. You start thinking you can't make it alone. You may be scared. But you're just as scared trying to figure out how to make it on your own. I had been a struggling single mother. I knew it was a battle, and by this time, was convinced the reason that I struggled before was because I was a failure. Eventually, during one of his out of town trips, I made a visit to a previous landlord, whom I actually called Grandma. We had grown quite close at one time, and she was more than glad to rent me one of her houses. I made the move. What should have been the end was far from over.

"Bad Root - No Good Fruit"

I landed a new position working a morning and midday show for an up and coming new contemporary adult format. We placed high on the Arbitron (Nielson type) ratings for a new station. Although I was no longer living with him, the interaction with this man continued, in a warped co-dependence. I would wash my hands of him, and then he'd come bearing gifts and money. Shortly after, the cycle of abuse would return. Bells really started to ring after a conversation with his mother. I had met her a year or so prior in his home state, but we were never left alone to speak, and it was an extremely short visit. When we were ready to leave, I thought it odd she would say, "You seem like a nice girl; be careful and good luck." Those words haunted me until we had a chance to speak again. She would later clarify the unimaginable. In a rare moment, he once dropped his guard with me, and told me about the abuse by his alcoholic stepfather. How he'd violently thrown him against the wall. How blood from his nose and lips had splattered, but he was ordered to clean it up.

I was living on my own, but the necessity of a vehicle and blatant lack of funds would hand him far more control than I'd have liked, through the purchase of a car. At any moment he could have thrown a wrench in the works, leaving me back at square one. I had stopped trusting God and people, yet again. I didn't feel I could face the criticism I may have received. I didn't want to be reminded of how guilty I felt for the choices I'd made, or the predicament I was in. I felt like I had to handle this mess on my own. What a joke.

More times than I care to remember, he would call demanding that I come over. He left message after message, each one more menacing and abusive than the other. He would then drive over to my house and beat on all the windows and doors, until someone either called the police, or I'd open the door to try and calm him down. After a while, there was no calming him down, and I genuinely began to fear that this would never end. Once the car was paid for and the title was clear, I was no longer under obligation. I am ashamed to say it was only then, when I began to aggressively bring things to light to the local police. I believed I could end this.

As I distanced myself, his anger and aggression grew. Although he would make hundreds of thousands of dollars at jobs, he would run through money like water. He began writing bad checks and defrauding clients of money. I kept records of every transaction that took place. When his mother and I talked, I felt the blood drain as she told me of his repeated psychiatric hospitalizations. She told me how he'd lied and fabricated documents about classes he'd taken. No bible school, no martial arts, no scuba instructor, and the list went on. I knew he'd been married before, but had very little information about it. She told me his marriage had ended very badly. She didn't know all the details but knew he'd gone to jail. She was told he had tried to burn the house down with his wife and her child from a previous marriage in it.

Back then we had no flat rate phone plans. Every long distance call had a toll. So I bought phone cards and when I went to work, would make calls and inquiries to every county I knew he'd lived in. One day I found out what I can only say left me shocked. I guess the deputy I spoke to could hear the desperation in my voice. She informed me there was usually a fee to obtain these records, but if I'd give her a fax number, she'd send them to me. There was charge after charge of domestic abuse, child endangerment, breaking restraining orders and so on. As I read, I became physically sick. I tried to bring this to the local police department's attention by speaking to an officer I knew. I begged for his discretion, and for him not to divulge what I had shared. Less than twenty four hours passed, when I began receiving the threatening phone calls from my ex. He told me to keep my mouth shut or he'd be sure to leave no evidence. Apparently the officer had not only broken my confidence, but had landed me in even more danger. How else could he have found out? It was during this time he had spoken with one of my friends on the phone, and told her if I made trouble for him, it would be very easy for him to take me up in his plane and drop me over a body of water, where no one would ever find me.

I began to reconnect with my friend from church. The same friend who had encouraged me to go out with him in the beginning. The irony is, I seemed to get more judgment and condemnation from this person, even though I was trying harder and harder to break free. I knew I'd messed up but was really trying hard to stop the madness. It would come to light much later on that her marriage was in trouble, and she and my "boyfriend" were spending more and more time talking on the phone.

I had left some things at his house and was resigned to the fact that it wasn't worth the risk of going back to retrieve them. Yet when he called, full of apologies, and offering to return my things, I was stunned. He talked of "meeting someone", that it was "time to move on". I was welcome to get my things and we would end this on a civil note. True, he had met someone else. In fact, many others. I was relieved he was ready to let it go, but everything in me screamed, don't go over there alone. I knew how fast his moods could swing and I wanted to seize the moment before it changed. The minute I walked through the door, I knew it was too late. With a gun in his hand, he marched me into the office and called my friend from church on speaker phone. She proceeded to regale him with every secret and confidence I'd told her regarding him. She was all too willing to reveal all she knew. I remember saying over and over, "You don't know what you've just done". I remember her saying something to the effect that I was being dramatic and needed to stop. I stood there crying, begging her to please stop talking. When the phone call ended, the abuse that would last all night began.

There are details far too graphic to share, but I was basically back in the attic again. When I was younger and I'd get upset crying, it would sometimes end in throwing up. One of the worse moments of that night, occurred after hours of crying from pain and abuse. I began to feel nauseated. Because he was very materialistic, he determined he wouldn't let me get sick on his expensive bed. He dragged me into the bathroom, sticking my head over the toilet. I had been hours without eating, and could only retch at this point. The gun that he had waved at me throughout the night, remained in his hand. For a moment, I thought it was ending and almost believed he showed compassion as he stroked the back of my head and said, "I find if you can't get sick, it helps to stick a finger down your throat." He then lifted my head, stuck the barrel of the gun in my mouth forcefully and said "Let me help. But I'm warning you, if you get sick on my gun, it will be the last thing you do." I am purposely omitting the expletives he frequently used. I had prayed all night for him to fall asleep, as he ranted and chain smoked between the physical and verbal abuse. I am grateful to be alive, for in that moment when that gun was in my mouth, I *did* get sick, and he *did* pull the trigger. We were both stunned when it only clicked. But I seized the moment, pushed him and ran. I locked myself in the office and was able to call the police. Guns were drawn and he was arrested. When the case finally went to court, I asked the judge to put him somewhere he would get help. But instead, he said, "I don't run a rehab. Case dismissed."

This was a town and a time that believed if you were in that sort of situation, you had asked for it. He truly had met another woman and eventually left the state. He was also wanted for check charges, so he didn't risk returning and hired movers to pack his belongings. They had no key to enter the premises, but I did. Many people will not understand why, when he contacted me to let them in and see all his belongings packed and carted away, I did. I was asked later by one of the police that knew this case, "Why would you do this?" My answer, "Once I saw for myself that it was packed, loaded, and on its way out of state, I could truly believe he was gone." I never saw or spoke to him again. I have moved from anger to compassion and forgiveness for this terribly broken man. I have prayed many times for his deliverance. My daughter informed me she later spoke with him again on Facebook. In a sarcastic remark, he commented to my daughter that he thought with all my talent, I would have by now made a mark. When my daughter and I discussed this, I assured her that *I* am not here to make a mark, but to be the instrument God *uses* to make his.

"Some Christians Are Like Bad Polaroids: Over Exposed and Underdeveloped"

I realize the enormity of my sins and just how much God has, and will, continue to forgive me for. We pray "Forgive us our trespasses as we forgive those who trespass against us." Really? Do we *really* want him to forgive us like we do others? I have to be sure, even when I'm tempted to hold a little something back that I know I *should* be giving to God, to remember this. I pray I will always forgive others the way he has forgiven me. You'd be surprised when you start to practice this, how determined you become to forgive, love, and offer compassion for those who have wronged you. There is no doubt that I had unresolved issues that I chose to ignore.

Stemming from childhood, the layers built up until I vowed I would never trust whole heartedly again. I longed for the relationship I once had with the Lord, but quite frankly could not feel any desire to draw in. As I said before, God gives us feelings and emotions with the intention of us ruling them, not the other way around. I had been hurt by people, but when it came from fellow Christians, it was the ultimate betrayal. I expected better. We have far too many walking wounded in churches today. Sadly, many of those wounds were inflicted inside the walls of a church. We have developed standards and measurements that people must meet to fit the "Jesus Club."

I am reminded of a story from my Daddy that speaks to this very subject. Many years ago, in the Deep South, a tired old black man was walking a hot dusty path. Weary from his burdens, he began to pray for God to give him strength to continue his journey. At that very moment, he began to hear the most heavenly voices singing Amazing Grace. As the sound grew nearer, a little white church began to appear on the horizon. Feeling the presence of God, his step quickened as he climbed the hill and eventually the steps of the church. Slipping in the door, he immediately noticed the contrast of dress. His worn dusty overalls stood out amongst the neatly pressed, ironed, and tailored clothes worn by the congregation. He resolved to blend into the pew and tried to remain unnoticed, merely wanting to participate in the worship. As he closed his eyes to pray, he felt a firm hand grip his shoulder. Looking up, he saw a rigid and authoritative deacon bend down and ask him to please leave. As despondence washed over him, he meekly and obligingly stepped out the door. Feeling worse than before, he paused briefly to sit and pray on the steps of the church. Again, he felt a firm hand grip his shoulder. Dreading to once again face the deacon, he slowly glanced upward only to see the magnificent face of Jesus. Jesus lovingly whispered to the old man, "Don't worry son. I've been trying to get into this church for years." It became one of the most valuable lessons my Daddy ever taught. The lesson is this: We need to please God, not people. We don't have to fit in a group or clique. Service will not save us, but we are saved to serve. But most of all, believe what God says about us, not man.

Over the next few years, figuratively speaking, I would occasionally surf the holy water but never felt excitement. My career had taken a turn, and I left radio to become a full time voice over artist. It eventually got to the point where my voice saturated the air waves over the southeast. I was the voice that answered one of the leading cell phone companies. My voice was on city and municipal directories. Talking fingers from the local phone company. Time and temperature, not to mention advertising numerous products on both radio and television. I auditioned for movie roles and worked for about a year as a comedian/singer at a two hour professional variety show. I wrote and created all the characters I performed. It's not surprising they worked so well, considering all the faces I'd lived behind for so many years. It was during this time I met my beloved husband. Past experiences made me extremely cautious, and I was very careful to wade in. We were friends first, and the relationship grew from that foundation. I am blessed to say many years of marriage later, he is still my best friend.

I've never known such patience, kindness, love, and endurance in one human being. I have to be honest and tell you, I'm sure the first couple of years we were married, he must have thought, "Oh lord, what have I done? This is not what I signed up for." There is a classic movie and song called, "Love Is A Many Splendored Thing." In my case, love was a many "Splintered" thing. This poor man must have thought I was into bird watching, because I watched him like a hawk, looking for failure and disappointment with every turn. When we first got married, we had a lot of words. Actually he had words, I had paragraphs. I was so confused about who I was and what I should be. I changed personalities and accents like changing clothes. I look back now and think how good it was that I was into acting, or I could have ended up in a padded cell. I was literally like Meryl Streep on steroids. Made for Hollywood. Speaking of Hollywood, the irony is, it was started around 1887, by a Kansas real estate tycoon, named Horace Wilcox. He developed it as a place for Midwesterners, who were fed up with winters and the cold snow. Saloons were banned, and free land was offered to anyone that wanted to come out and start a church. These days it sometimes feels like they'll offer a Christian land if they'll move out.

Getting back to the story, you never knew day to day what you got with me. In the first few years of our marriage, my husband never knew what woman he would wake up beside. Niki nice, or Niki not so nice. Niki know it all, or Niki numb. My husband is a constant, methodical, patient man, which is part of what drew me to him. I had lived through enough chaos for the both of us. However, until I got rid of a few demons and a whole lot of Samsonite, there were things about that calm that drove me crazy. My husband is the kind of man that can tell you off in such a nice way, you actually end up thanking him for doing it. Not me! I blew through like a Nor'easter leaving wounded and casualties everywhere I went. If it didn't go the way I wanted it, look out. I would drive like every place was the last place on earth I'd ever see. Not my husband. He'd let people pull out in front of him, drove the speed limit, didn't honk the horn, and I'd get so frustrated riding with him I'd feel my whole body shaking. You see, it was a control thing. The problem being, I didn't have any.

The longer I lived with his patience and his constant example of what I wasn't, it made me want to be a better person. But listen, living with a person that's a good example doesn't change you. It may eventually mirror your bad habits. But it can only be through God that makes it a permanent change. When we are wounded, we often put expectations on people to behave like we want them to, then criticize them when they don't. I was extremely harsh when people didn't meet my expectations or messed up, never considering how many I had missed, in the eyes of God. When people hurt us, we are well within our rights to tell them. But it must always be in love and with mercy. Otherwise, it's just anger or emotions. We have to be able to see ourselves through God's eyes, not always as a victim.

Most of the time what really needs fixing is not what is going on around you but what's inside you. In my case, I was constantly raising the bar for what I thought it would take to make me happy. I would ask my husband for nice jewelry, bigger diamonds, nice home, and nice cars to drive. Although there was a temporary thrill, it would always fade. Nothing made me happy. That's not surprising because I had a God sized need, and was trying to fill it with a man sized solution. When you find peace, you tend to be less critical. You stop looking for fault in others. One of the worst faults we all have is to think we don't have any.

 I used to be horrible about poor food service. I still prefer an attentive and kind food server. But if my food was not prepared correctly, or if I wasn't treated the way I expected, I would leave about an inch of you standing, after tearing strips out of you with my mouth. When I began to look at these things through the eyes of Jesus, what used to be an impolite or miserable waitress or cashier, began to look like a worn out single mom, whose eyes were dull because she was ending or starting a second or third job. Perhaps what little sleep she got was interrupted by a sick child crying all night, or an abusive or drunk spouse. Maybe she had her own addictions, and was hanging by her fingernails to find a reason not to end it all at the end of her shift. Perhaps she was dreading going back to the shelter, safe house, or sleeping in her car. When you think about it that way, they are no longer the horrible waiter or waitress. They're a human being that has crossed your path and it's amazing what can we do to change the perspective of this person's day, possibly their life.

Proverbs 18:21 says "Death and life are in the power of the tongue, and they that love it shall eat the fruit thereof." I had to become completely transparent before God, about who I was, and who I'd been, for things to change. I recall having a conversation with God while standing in front of the mirror one day. As I was thinking about the saying, "Loose lips sink ships," God gently reminded me my tongue had been a torpedo. I had wounded many. I can honestly say it was the love of Jesus that taught me, marriage is a duet, not a duel. Old fears and lack of trust reared its ugly head from time to time. My inability to believe or trust a man made it difficult to accept my husband wouldn't bail, or be pushed away out of true love and commitment to me. It was incomprehensible. In time, his example of true and lasting love made it possible for the walls to drop.

Again, I was still wrestling with the desire to be a good Christian, yet sitting in church feeling dull and blunted. Would I ever feel spiritual joy again? I'm reminded of a personal experience where God was able to break a constant cycle of worry and fear in my own life.

As you have read, there were many areas where the enemy had fertile soil to plant memories and thoughts. He reminded me not only of abuses I had endured, but bad choices I had made. When we live in regret, we cannot move forward, and are often paralyzed by recycling these images over and over in our head. There are two memories that held me as captive as any physical chain that was ever on my body. How dominating these thoughts were, especially at night. Almost like clockwork, as soon as the lights were off, my mind became a screen flooded with these images. I'd try to watch TV to drown them out and still they were there. I'd read my bible, but returned to these thoughts, and I would have to reread the page over and over as nothing got though. This was a ritual that repeated every night, and I would sincerely pray for God to remove this guilt and shame. Still it continued. One of these memories involved my daughter and the guilt I felt of what she'd been exposed to.

It would be accurate to say my daughter understands grooming. During my involvement and relationship with my last abuser, my daughter began to display very unhealthy behavior. She was not only defiant, as most teenage girls can be, but abusive. I felt a lot of guilt for the amount of anger I held towards her. It was towards the end of this relationship with him, the preview of my later medical mysteries began. Although my hospitalizations were in no way as frequent as they would become later, the severity of the illness was beginning to emerge. I would spend at least two weeks in the hospital, on two or three separate occasions. You see, I was not the only one he dangled money and worldly goods in front of. As music has been my siren as a teenager, money and flashy cars were my daughter's. He would buy her cars and in doing so, buy her loyalty. There was more than once, whether I was in the hospital or recovering at home, she would not call or visit for days. I would try to have the authorities bring her home, and would always hit a dead end.

As in my own teenage years, she began to lie to cover her bases. To explain her behavior, she lied about things I'd supposedly said or done. Betrayal hurts in any form, but nothing hurts like the betrayal of a child. Those wounds cut deep and the cycle was repetitive. You see, when I didn't feel heard as a child, my resentment grew and wedges were formed between my Mama and me. When my daughter was little and I didn't listen, I suppose the same seed was planted. By the time I was listening, she was no longer talking. I made enough mistakes on my own, I certainly didn't need the embellishments.

Still, as I had learned too late, "mud sticks." There are those who still choose to believe tales, rather than truth. This was one of the memories that I wrestled with every night. Would I ever be validated? What part had I played in this behavior? Had more happened to her than I knew? Had she been damaged by secrets, lies, and shame, the way I'd been as a teenager? Was she, like I had been, willing to take it to the grave rather than feel others' contempt and judgment?

The other memory I will not share. I am still processing things that have happened in my life, though I am not controlled by them. Perhaps this would be a good place to say, never insist that a survivor share their story. The key words here; *"THEIR STORY!"* I have given all my hurts to God and may be scarred, but not scabbed. I know it happened, I have chosen to surrender all. Too often, I will hear women say, "I just want to be normal." I used to feel the same way, until it finally dawned on me that "normal" is merely a setting on your dryer. We will never be normal, but we can all aspire to be healthy.

Years later, while traveling out of town for my daughter's surgery, I remember pulling up to the hotel where I would be staying. As I glanced up the wall of the hotel, scanning the windows, all I could think of was "here we go again." I sat in the car, and began to pray out loud, "I have given this to you over and over and you don't take it away." Why? It was at that moment, I felt the Holy Spirit speak clearly into my heart, "Because you believe your emotions, more than you believe me." I can truthfully say that was the last time I was ever tormented with those thoughts again.

Do I care about my daughter and her journey? Absolutely! I love my daughter dearly and speak God's grace over her life. But I cannot hand everything to God and then get in the way of what he may need to do in her life. There has been tremendous healing, but as in my own life, he is not done. It's not my job to determine her steps, only to pray over them. We overcome by the "Christ in you", not "Christ plus you." It took forever to write my own book, so I'm surely not going to try and rewrite God's!

"Tough Times Never Last – Tough People Do"

Around 1999, early 2000, I had been experiencing a progression of serious health issues. At first, I dismissed it as stress, life changes, diet and various causes. I eventually could no longer ignore the pain and fatigue, and sought medical help. I'd had some previous GI issues and sincerely believed this was the explanation. I could have been knocked over with a feather, when my primary doctor came back with a diagnosis of liver disease.

In the past I had only been a social drinker, and had quit drinking all together by this time. Without delving into too many details, I will tell you I went through two rounds of chemotherapy to try and harness the illness into remission. It was also suggested that my gallbladder be removed, to make room for my swelling liver. This was done as an outpatient procedure, and I was released to recover at home. Although the treatment normalized the liver enzymes and swelling was reduced, I continued to have abdominal and upper right quadrant pain that never seemed to subside. I once asked the surgeon, "If the gallbladder is gone and the liver is no longer presenting threats, why do I feel worse? " His explanation? I was, "most likely having phantom pain." I'm aware when you've had extremities removed, arms, legs, fingers, toes, etc., there are cases of this. I remember my own grandmother having her legs amputated from raging diabetes and talking how her missing limbs hurt and itched. I'd never heard of phantom pain from a gall bladder. I wasn't a surgeon and therefore accepted the explanation.

Time went on, and the pain worsened. The need for relief grew. I went from having doctor visits for occasional pain medicine, to being admitted to hospital every three to four months and eventually once a month or more. I was diagnosed with everything from bowel obstructions to diverticulitis, ulcerative colitis to visceral pain. I began to see a primary doctor who was quite busy, but willing to take me as a patient and as he put it, "provide me pain relief until we had some answers." From the first office visit, he prescribed 100mg Demerol injections to be self-administered at home, as well as 60mg of oxycodone. I began to immediately sink into an angry and confused state that only deepened into dark depression. This prescriptive cocktail continued to increase as did my symptoms and illness, not to mention my dependence on these medicines. They sure got it right calling it pain medicine. I was not only trying to medicate the physical pain, but block out the emotional pain that had been layering for years. I believe wholeheartedly that addicts are merely trying to self-medicate in the beginning. By the time you realize you have an addiction, there is no real relief, only the suspension of the inevitable events that will have to take place to be free of the addiction.

You'll never find an addict who clearly knows they have a problem and say "I like where I am and I want to stay here the rest of my life." Quite the opposite. Most will tell you they'd give anything to be free of the day to day slavery they endure. It's the fear of what it will take that hinders the steps to recovery. It's hoping to avoid the unknown pain to come. Many stay in this situation, because even though it's pain, it's still pain they know.

When the news of Michael Jackson's death became public knowledge, many were outraged at how he died. Many were confused how anything like overdosing in the presence of a doctor could *even* happen. I did not share the same shock, not because it wasn't appalling, but because I had experienced a very similar situation. There were many times when I was at the absolute worst, and by all accounts should have been admitted to the hospital. My primary at the time would send home health care nurses to start an IV, and leave me to administer the Demerol without supervision.

It is truly the grace of God I was not a fatality. When pain speaks, it gets your attention, and will often dictate over ethics, wisdom, or safety. The more my husband and I pleaded for answers, the higher the dosage of the prescription would go. I don't think the magnitude of how close to the edge I came actually dawned on me, until I was donating the IV pole to Hospice, cleaning the bags of empty bottles, Demerol boxes, and sharps containers, out of my house. This was only the last six months of usage, and yet the quantity could have easily medicated the outpost of a war zone. In fact, a doctor had even at one point stated, he didn't know how I was still breathing with the amount of narcotics in my system. I was on 100mg of Demerol I.M. every 2 hours, 60mg of Roxicodone every 2-4 hours, 180 mg of OxyContin twice a day and 2mg of Xanax twice a day. A dangerous cocktail indeed!

This went on for about four years. I literally lived in my bed. As far as I was concerned, life as I knew it was over. I had cried until I could no longer cry. I prayed until I could no longer pray. I went from lying in bed watching TV, to just staring at the walls. It's incredible the amount of narcotics I was on, and yet I would sometimes go for days without sleeping. The insomnia was awful. I began to wish that if things didn't change, I'd rather just die. Soon I began to pray to die. When that didn't happen, I began to think of taking matters into my own hands. I was so sick of this endless cycle of pain, nausea, vomiting, and hospitalizations. During those days of lying in bed and staring at the walls, I remember thinking I wanted to be anywhere else and anyone else, but me. I look back and wonder if I truly believed God heard my prayers. We throw out the term, "I'll pray for you" so loosely, but do we really believe it? I would be remiss if I didn't share the story of how some Christians truly perceive prayer.

A church, in a small community in eastern Tennessee, was outraged when a local businessman built a bar right across the street. For months, they battled with city hall and town meetings in hopes of having the bar closed. The church was adamant that on Wednesday and Sunday nights, the whooping and hollering that came from the parking lot, was found to be extremely offensive to the congregation. The congregation launched into a month of weekly prayer services for God to remove this bar. After one of the worst storms in Tennessee history, the bar was struck by lightning and burned to the ground. The celebration was short lived when the bar's owner presented a suit that the church's prayers had cost his business. Upon reviewing the arguments in court, from both sides, the judge stated, "I don't know what has confused me more: The church that claims their prayers weren't answered or the bartender who claims they were?"

Don't most of us ask God for something, with the answer already in mind? We get terribly offended, even though we pray for his will, when it doesn't turn out as we expect. With that being said, are we truly praying or merely complaining? If it's not the content, it's the method. Most of us have been taught we must stand on ceremony when speaking to God. True, we must revere him. But we should be able to go to him comfortably and speak as the dearest of friends. He is our father. Our heavenly father. I don't know about you, but when I talked to my Daddy, I didn't say, "Oh Nathaniel, son of Ernest, father of Nicole, hearest my plea." If I was in trouble, I just yelled, "DADDY!!!", and he'd come running. I'm sure when God hears "thees" and "thous", he probably smiles with a forgiving, but comical grin. Do we really believe he talks this way? I think it's safe to say, he speaks our language. After all, he created it.

"Don't Pray For Rain If You Can't Stand the Mud"

Along with the abdominal issues, I began to have serious joint pain. Strange rashes appeared on my face, arms, and chest, but by the time I could get in to the doctor, it would be cleared up. When no obstructions showed up on CT scans, the doctors would treat me like I was drug seeking. It's bad enough to hurt and be sick, but to feel like you must defend yourself in the midst of this can really knock you back. This increased the depression. Along with the constant pain and need for pain relief, I was always defending myself. I became enveloped by the darkness. At one point, a less than subtle doctor told me I was depressed and needed to get over it in front of a group of medical students. This humiliating remark took me right back to the days of abuse, where I'd been belittled so horribly.

Between admissions, I withdrew from answering the phone. I didn't call and speak with my family. I retreated to bed and settled back into staring at the wall. I would pray repeatedly, "God please help me. This cannot be what you want for my life. This cannot be all there *is* to my life. Please God, please." I couldn't plan anything without factoring in the risk of a hospitalization. I couldn't plan trips, let alone go out for meals. There was usually a high risk of me getting sick. In addition to the complications, a diagnosis of diabetes was given.

During this time, there were people who would call, "encouraging me" and yet rarely did. I'm sure they meant well. I can remember hearing things like "God's got a plan" or "He won't give you more than you can bear." The worst one was "I know just how you feel." I wanted to scream, "No! You Don't!" Don't ever tell someone you know *just* how they feel. I, like them, also used to say these things.

Mama and I both deal with GI issues. One day, while she was updating me on her doctor's visit, she informed me the doctor had diagnosed her with diverticulitis. Listen, by now I was the poster child for GI issues. So, I quickly added, "I know just how you feel." The Lord later spoke to me and convicted me that I needed to apologize to her. You see, I may have known what it was like to experience this as a 20, 30, 40, and 50 plus individual. But, I have not arrived to my 80's yet. So,

I can't possibly know "just" how she felt. It's okay to say "I relate" or "I've had something that sounds similar." But, we need to try and stay away from comparisons. When someone is going through trials, it's even okay to say, You know, I've never been where you are and I'm not going to pretend to be the expert, but in my own life, this is what God brought me through." Be sure, however, we are encouraging and not comparing. People with sympathy addictions hate when others are in the spotlight. Sometimes, we really should just pray without announcing it.

Years before, while living in Greenville, South Carolina, my daughter and I spent many weekends at the Biltmore Estate in Asheville, North Carolina. My parents went with us on one occasion, and we made some wonderful memories viewing the house and grounds. We visited the surrounding mountain town, Saluda, and Daddy talked of wanting to live closer to us and having the mountains as his back yard. After my Daddy died, Mama and I often talked of going back. After she survived pancreatic cancer, I knew we needed to do more than just talk.

Although I was becoming more ill, I became more determined I would not give up on God bringing me through. Mama, I and my oldest granddaughter scheduled a Biltmore excursion. I drove to Rocky Mount to spend the night and planned to drive the following day to Asheville. In hindsight, probably not the best plan when you're being admitted in hospitals on a biweekly basis. I arrived at the hotel miserably sick and couldn't emerge from the hotel bed the entire next day. The following day we set out for Asheville as planned.

All the way there, I struggled with stomach pains, nausea, cramping, and aching joints. I had barely eaten. Mama couldn't understand why I was so irritable and just wanted to be quiet. It felt like land mines were going off in my gut. The next morning at the hotel, I could barely tolerate the smell of food, although I had been looking forward to the breakfast at this Inn from a previous stay. It continued to worsen. We barely made it to the second floor at Biltmore when I turned ghostly white. I was sweaty and nauseated, and every joint and muscle screamed in my body. Mama finally said, "Let's just go" to

81

everyone's disappointment. When we returned to the car, all I could do was lean on the steering wheel and pray. All the way home, I frequently stopped to be sick. I don't know of any trips I've experienced that have been more miserable. I returned to the hotel in Rocky Mount and didn't emerge for two days, until I couldn't take it anymore. I called my daughter and asked her if she'd please go with me to the emergency room. I was admitted for a partial bowel obstruction, but they couldn't tell me why. I was there for more than a week and left none the wiser, but just as miserable.

This cycle would continue over and over, in and out of the hospital. More and more pain medications became necessary until I hit an emotional brick wall. I began to talk to God earnestly and honestly about my life, my situation, and my health. What was happening to me? I didn't have the answers, but I knew God did. I began to get clarity on many things. I had been begging for God to help all of this time, when he'd already given me tools I needed. I'd been waiting for him to do all the work. God knows our heart. In reality, if he'd performed a miracle, I would have expected him to continue the parlor tricks again and again. I would have relied on an emotional experience to get me through tough times. He knew I needed to start the walk of faith.

The first step of this walk was to get the narcotics out of my body. No one was going to take me seriously with these pain medicines. I had to taper off. Only then, would someone take me seriously about what was going on. I needed a clear head and the ability to explain my symptoms without the fog of narcotics masking my words.

God will often give us the nuggets we need to push beyond where we are. I've read John 19:30 hundreds of times. I remember clearly the day I read it again and heard the Holy Spirit say, Jesus said, "It is finished" not I am finished. I've learned there's a big difference between finished and complete. What the enemy sent to finish me, God will use to complete me. The word tells us that the enemy roams to and fro, like a lion seeking whom it may devour. For those in Christ, the good news is, the enemy may be "like a lion", but we have "THE" lion of Judah for every need. It was a defining moment that said nothing or no one could stop what God has started. I was determined not to be the woman who died at thirty, but buried at eighty. Every man will die, but not every man lives.

We often give up because we have no vision. We say things like, "I just don't see how I'm ever going to get better". That clearly states we have no vision. Habakkuk 2:3 says, "For the vision is yet for an appointed time and it hastens till the end fulfillment. It will not deceive or disappoint, though it tarries, wait earnestly for it. It will not be behindhand on its appointed day."

I'm reminded of the Impala, the animal that can jump as high as ten feet, as long as thirty feet. Yet if you put it behind a fence of only four feet in height, it won't even attempt to jump, because it can't see what's ahead. How often do we fence ourselves in because we're afraid of what's ahead in life? When I finally realized all that I had left was God, it became apparent he was all I ever needed.

"Swallow Your Pride - It Won't Make You Fat"

I began what I called God's detox. Most 60 to 90 day rehabs focus on cognitive behavior. I vowed for sixty days I would only read my bible, Christian authors, listen to Christian music and Christian teachings. I would spend a lot of time getting honest with God about my thoughts, my behavior, my pain, my hurts, and my cover-ups. That was some time ago, but as a result, I have learned how important what we watch, listen to, and read impacts us. I literally watch approximately two percent secular programming. I'm very careful about what goes in.

During the following months, I changed my attitude, my gratitude, and all my food. The diabetes became totally controlled by diet. We can't sit around and pray for God to do this and do that, doing nothing, expecting things to happen. Even with positive changes, the stomach pain, fatigue, joint pain and skin rashes continued to increase. In 2010, I remember praying, "God, let this year be the year of information and validation. No matter what, I will still serve you and give you praise. Please God, lead me to the right people."

The GI group I'd been seeing for some time hired a new addition to the practice. I believe they'd done their best, but now a fresh pair of eyes began looking at my history. A former naval doctor, with a heart of gold, took this case like a soldier intending to win the battle. Around this same time, my new Primary sent me to a specialist to rule out anything infectious. Trying to explain the rashes and swellings was so frustrating. I began to document with pictures. I photographed the rashes on my face, neck, chest and arms. My eyes would get painful and bloodshot. My hands and joints would swell and redden. After some in-depth tests, he suggested I see a rheumatologist. He thought the pictures and symptoms sounded a great deal like the rare autoimmune disorder Dermatomyositis. It's best described as a cross between Lupus and Muscular Dystrophy. The advanced stage has resulted in paralysis, being unable to breathe, eventually leading to death. Little did I know my prayer for information was about to be answered. What seemed like two different conditions, abdominal and arthritic, would be connected more than imagined.

In September 2010, I was admitted again with bowel obstruction, nausea, vomiting and severe pain, this time, with my new GI as attending physician. While there, the Malar or butterfly rash became visible on my face. My hip and knee joints were so painful, I required a cane to walk. For the first time in years, someone finally saw this wasn't about pain medicine, but pain. After a week, I was released, receiving IV treatment with home health nurses for an additional week. In October, my GI ordered a specialized CT scan. I wasn't sure it would give any more answers than all the previous tests. What an ambivalent feeling, when the tests came back showing two areas of growths in my small bowel; right where I'd been complaining of pain all this time. Ambivalent in the sense, something had finally appeared, and yet, what did it mean? He referred me to a local surgeon, who reviewed the scan and my health history. He was very honest when he said it would be very risky to have another bowel resection (this would be my 4th). He thought it was "a potential fire storm waiting to happen," with all the healing issues. Especially the autoimmune. If you keep removing bowel, you'll eventually run out. As I said before, my GI was no quitter and he already had plan B.

There's a specialized procedure called a Double Balloon Enteroscopy. Specialized in the sense, it is not without risks. Most common, bowel perforation. The ability to travel the entire intestinal tract and remove abnormalities with someone whose healing is compromised by traditional surgery, is where the benefit outweighs the risk. He referred me to a Naval colleague at a well-known cancer clinic in Philadelphia. This surgeon had quite the resume, including his time on the medical staff at the White House. His kind and unassuming nature never gave it away.

There would be two procedures, the first on the Tuesday before Christmas. I'd been warned that you sometimes wake with extreme discomfort, and so I was a bit nervous going in. My husband videoed the first day, including recovery. I had never dreamed during surgery before, but as I slipped into unconsciousness, I stepped into the most incredible dream I'd ever had. I began to dream Jesus was standing behind me, with his arms extended around in front of me. He appeared so large, and I was childlike and enfolded in his arms. It was so peaceful, and I can tell you I felt no fear. I kept trying to turn around and look him in the face, but he kept turning me back and would gently say, "It's not time to see my face yet, but I have you. I'm holding you and it's all right." I remember the hands being crossed in front of me and the scars. The scars were not in his palms, or his wrists, but where the palm meets wrist. The scars were cross shaped, as though the nails were four sided. As I woke in recovery, the camera was rolling. I immediately began telling my husband about seeing Jesus. Oh, how I wanted to go back to sleep and see him again! It then occurred to me, I felt no pain. Not one bit. A few minutes later the doctor came in and said, "We saw nothing. Everything looks normal, but we still have tomorrow." I was released back to the hotel where we were staying. I slept the better part of the day and night, but no more dreams of Jesus.

The next morning I woke with the old familiar gnawing pain and nausea I'd had for so long. We returned to registration, and I was again prepped for the procedure. The pain and nausea worsened. The anesthesiologist came over, and we discussed how well the day before had gone. I was so disappointed the pain was back. The pain caused my blood pressure to elevate, and it was recommended they medicate me before taking me back. I was rolled back into the same suite from the day before, sedated, and the room went dark. This time, no peaceful dreams, and when I awoke, it was anything but pain free: A complete contrast from the day before. I retched with nausea and was wracked with pain. After the procedure, I don't remember who initiated the conversation but was told they were going to admit me and give me more information when I was more alert and comfortable.

The next day, the surgeon came to my hospital room to share his findings. He shared how they'd been confident from the first procedure going so well, that nothing would turn up. As they were ending the procedure, he had dismissed the resident. But, just as he was leaving the room, the surgeon called him back and said, "You have got to see this." This surgeon had seen many things, but as he told my husband and me, this was the craziest thing he had ever seen. Apparently during a surgery many years before, the stitching had been done incorrectly, and loops of suture now hung loosely inside my

86

bowel. In addition, they had left a piece of gauze which was now embedded in my bowel. I don't think I realized exactly what he was saying, until he showed me the pictures and report, showing the foreign body near the duodenum/jejunum area. All these years of being told it was all in my head that I was exaggerating, drug seeking. I was finally vindicated. God keeps his word. Sometimes we aren't happy with the time line, but he keeps his word!

The final six months of bottles and boxes. The two white bags are full of empty Demerol boxes.

Note the different sizes of sharps containers. The larger one came up to my waist and was full of empty cartridges and used needles.

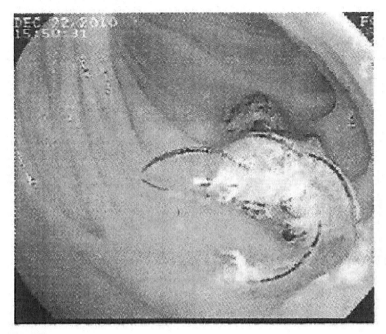

1 Foreign Body

The area of foreign body found during the procedure in Philadelphia. The large white spot is the gauze and the black lines are loops of suture.

"Even Good Seasons Have Bad Weather"

There were so many doctors who were sure they were right. I had a divine incident with one of these doctors. Remember the one I'd mentioned earlier, that had insulted me in front of the students? I had an opportunity to meet him again one day on the elevator while visiting with the hospital ministry team. I began to tell him about the findings, and how God is good. He rolled his eyes and said, "Oh you're one of those." At this point, I reminded him that he was a doctor who had studied medicine and wholeheartedly believed in the tests that told him nothing was wrong with me. I then asked, "If you are so wrong about something you know so much about, how much more wrong might you be about the existence of the creator?" He stepped off the elevator without a word, but there had been another doctor riding with us. As I began to step out on the floor, the other doctor turned to me and said, "You've made me think today." I now realize my witness wasn't for the doctor who insulted me, but the doctor on the elevator with us. I am humbled that God thought me worthy to use in some way, to help this man seek truth.

Once my rheumatologist got the report, you could almost see the light bulb in her head. Prior to this, she'd also done several tests, one being a DNA that checks if this particular autoimmune had been inherited. There are two ways that increase your risk for autoimmune disorders, inherited and environmental. Environmental meaning medications and exposures to certain things. Mine was negative for inherited. She explained my body had been fighting for years. Trying to rid itself of this foreign body, thinking it was an infection. Basically overworking itself, fighting against this gauze and sutures. She then diagnosed me with reactive arthritis and sclerodactyly, which makes writing and typing extremely painful from the tightening of the skin. I thank God for the hands of a volunteer, who typed my dictation so I could tell my story the way God would have it told.

With this diagnosis, I began to pray specifically. I believed that God would give me the strength to get up out of bed every day and keep moving. He has honored his word. He gets me up every single day, and I now minister to people, something I would never have thought possible. I have learned about far more than just medical mysteries. I've learned how to completely trust God. How to forgive. That I have far more to be happy about, than not. What used to feel like being sentenced to suffer, is now my opportunity to serve him. I've learned I can live through anything and still keep my joy. I have faith that if healing is not today, there's always tomorrow. Every morning is a new day to thank him for his goodness, his mercy, his love. A new opportunity to help others know the same loving God that always loved me. As I wrote in one of my songs, "When darkness fills my land, it's just the shadow of your mighty hand."

Doctors give prognoses but I have no problem telling them, I know a man! I believe his word more than theirs. For whatever reason, God may not choose to change my circumstances. What is more important, is that he has changed me. We get so caught up in our past and our hurts. Here's the thing. I have learned it's easier to pull people out of the past, than pull the past out of them. We get frustrated because we want to go back and change things. But as Joel 2:25 tells us, "I will repay you for the years the locusts have eaten." It doesn't mean these horrible things that happened to me didn't happen. They did. I now consider it as boot camp, training that I need for today.

"It's No Good to sit up and Take Notice If You Just Keep Sitting"

God has given me the opportunity to minister to women, in a way that takes the "You don't understand" card off the table. I am the founder of STAAR Ministry, (Stop The Abuse And Rescue). We're the only safe house in Pinellas County, Florida, as of this writing. It's aptly called Chrissie's House, after the brave and amazing woman who was part of my rescue. She sheltered me with unconditional love. I couldn't think of any name more appropriate, given all she'd done for me. As we are completely donor supported, we are thankful each day the doors are open. It is heartbreaking the amount of needs that come forward and yet how few volunteer, or commit financially to help. But as long as we are able to meet the needs, no one will ever be turned away.

Florida may be called the Sunshine State, but I have seen a lot of darkness. S.T.A.A.R. works tirelessly, to help women that have been trafficked, exploited and abused, to find freedom from their horrific pasts, to find recovery. But most of all, to meet Jesus. Most people would never form a corporation at my age. Most people are starting to think about retirement. Time is a blip on God's radar. If we believe his word, then we don't choose when we are no longer useful or when he can no longer *use* us. When we stay submissive, he does amazing things with a willing vessel. Sometimes we confuse what ministry looks like. I remember my daughter once excitedly proclaiming, "I believe God has called me to go overseas for ministry." To which I replied, "Make sure you can cross an aisle to help someone, before you cross an ocean."

We must first *Be* Jesus, before we convince people to *serve* Jesus. You may say I'm only one person. But one person named Hitler, caused millions of people pain. Good or evil, every thought starts with one person. Make a difference in just one person's life, preferably someone that will never thank you. We have to stop walking in rooms with the "Here I am" attitude and instead think "There you are."

As of now, I still have some physical hurdles to jump. I don't understand why God has not chosen to take all of the physical ailments away. I only know he promised to carry me, not explain it. I also know when I've reached the end of my rope, I only need to reach for the hem of his garment. He has promised me healing; he just never specified on which side I would get it. There was every rational excuse to never start this ministry. It would only dredge up memories, those memories that I had fought hard to keep a secret. I can recall when the story broke of the girls in Ohio, I was visiting family in North Carolina. It was hard to avoid. Every TV in the hotel where I stayed was blasting it 24/7. My precious friend, Donna, who had long known my story, would call me constantly to make sure I was ok. The similarities, you couldn't ignore. She worried it would trigger me back to the moment of my own ordeal. I won't pretend there weren't a few times I would have to catch my breath. But it only instilled that fire to fight for women who live this every day. We have horrendous stories, but they're not unique. There are women and men in chains right at this moment all around the world, possibly in your backyard.

For all intents and purposes, I've been labeled physically disabled, and I was far from financially sound to meet the needs. But as you may remember in previous chapters, God used David. You may also remember, as I pointed out, he was voted least likely to succeed by his father and brothers. God can build a "David" out of anyone that's obedient. But that's the vital ingredient. Obedience. S.T.A.A.R Ministry supports, shelters, and gives wrap-around services to victims and survivors of emotional, physical, and verbal abuse and human trafficking. These women are loved and nurtured by women who have walked where they've been, and are glad to guide them to a better place in life. It's not easy, and the challenges are many.

Not bad for a so called messed up, crippled, confused, old country gal, eh? I assure you, it is not me, but God. I am simply his instrument. In fact, if I had listened to doctors, this book would not exist. There are many reasons people would justify not taking this on. When God asked me to write this book, for a moment, I thought, "You've seen my hands. You know me. Are you serious?" Every ghost writer I spoke with, there was always a reason it didn't work out. It became blatantly clear the assignment was mine. It may have taken the time it took to write War and Peace. But as you have read, it includes a bit of war and ends with a lot of peace. We can do ALL things through Christ who strengthens us! Even write books with crippled hands. Even love girls the world has thrown away. We're all called to be in God's army.

I cannot close this book without yet another one of my Daddy's hilarious tales. We were exiting church one Sunday morning when our Pastor spoke to the young man in front of us notorious for only attending Christmas and Easter. The pastor clapped him on the shoulder and said, "Son, it's time for you to join God's army." The young man replied, "Pastor, I *AM* in God's army." At which point, my Daddy turned to me and whispered, "He must be Secret Service." My Daddy had much wisdom, and taught me many valuable lessons about life. I remember so clearly, as a child, walking the fields with him and stepping over to the abandoned grave site on our farm. Inspecting the old headstones, my Daddy solemnly questioned me, "What was the most important thing on the headstone?" Names? Births? Deaths? All to which he shook his head, "No." Surely there was nothing left and yet my Daddy pointed at the dash between the names and said, "This mark represents everything a man stands for in his life. Make sure your dash counts." We learn to hate far too easily; we judge someone by the color of their skin. But as my Daddy also said, "There's only one race. It's called the human race."

Sometimes my life has felt more confusing than road construction on Interstate 95. It doesn't make sense. There are delays; there are accidents. But when it's all finished and completed through God, it all comes together. I realize these things were necessary for God to work in my life. The hardest part is putting my trust in him *when* there's construction. The best explanation I've ever heard regarding trusting Jesus, is comparable to a parachute. You know they work, but do you really trust it will carry you when you jump from a plane? The difference is, Jesus never fails to carry. I recently found out the word parachute is from the French derivative para meaning shield and chute meaning fall. In other words, Jesus shields you from your falls. People who get impatient for God to answer actually lack humility. They've been deceived into believing they're too important to wait for God. Faith is not believing that God can; it's knowing God will.

"It's Not Our Place to See Through One Another - But See One Another Through"

In closing, I would like to share about someone I consider a real life hero. His name is Retired Rear Admiral Robert Shumaker. He was shot down in Vietnam and captured by the North Vietnamese. He spent eight years in different prisoner of war camps, including the Hoa Lo prison camp, which he dubbed the "Hanoi Hilton". He talks of the torture, in his words, "that would make you condemn your grandmother" where they tied a rope to his handcuffs, pulled it over his shoulders, and bent him down till his head touched his feet. He talks about screams, and how they were muffled by iron bars stuffed down their throats. For three years, he and eleven others were held in solitary cells, with no windows. Just a light bulb that hung over their heads that burned 24/7.

He would spend 10 to 12 hours a day imagining the house that he would build for him and his family, upon his return. His dream was so vivid, he knew it would require 5227 nails to put it together. Even in total isolation, he and the other men began to develop what became known as the tap code on the wall, which consisted of five letters and five columns. They began to communicate with one another so well, they managed to tap out French lessons, how to fix a TV, music lessons, and biology lessons. When they interviewed him later for a particular documentary, the first thing he demonstrated was how to tap out "God bless you".

A doctor at Mount Sinai Medical Center, who's had at least fifteen years' experience interviewing people who've endured terrible traumas, spoke about what all the most resilient and happy people have in common: Strong religious beliefs, moral beliefs, and strong role models. He noted that these people were not unaware of what happened to them, or even the magnitude of it, but always believed no matter what, they would prevail.

Shumaker's wife had not heard her husband's voice or seen him for eight years. She wasn't sure what kind of person would be coming back to her. Despite everything he'd gone through, his wife says the first phone call between them after his release erased all her fears. She knew the same man she married would be coming home. When asked, he has no problem saying that he grew from that experience. Given the opportunity, he would not have avoided it. He never would have learned the things that made him who he is today. He gained tools and found one doesn't need everything they think they do to be truly happy in this life. Oh, and just for the record, the house he imagined building now stands in Virginia. With all 5227 nails.

There is nothing that can prevent you from believing in your transformation, your miracle, but you! You have never endured more than God can heal. The choice is entirely up to you. Many people have overcome what the world deems as obstacles, but with the right attitude and persistence, it's really been opportunity. Daddy used to say, "No one can make you feel bad about yourself without your permission." I'm constantly reminded each time I remember his quotes or sayings that I don't know where they originated. But what impresses me the most is how many he had to have remembered. You see, he struggled with reading. It's amazing how he retained so much from just memory. He could have felt defeated and hard done by, because he'd lived in a time that required him to work on the farm. He didn't have the luxury of continuing his education, and yet it never stopped him from being a hard working husband and father, who was loved and respected by many. He was honest and always believed the naked truth is always better than a well-dressed lie.

Don't let meager or hurtful beginnings limit your potential. Decide today whether you will live scabbed or scarred. Scars are a reminder of things that have happened, but they no longer hurt. Scabs, on the other hand, never heal. They hurt as long as we pick at them, and continue to fester. I remained angry and relived horrible events, over and over, until the day I asked God to take those memories away. We have to choose which bridges to burn and which one to cross. I chose the one built with two boards and three nails, and I've never looked back. It only makes sense to complete this final chapter with a few more of Daddy's sayings. Daddy used to say, "If you fall down seven times, you get up eight. "There may be many reasons to act bad, but never good excuses." "Adversity is not always a bad thing. A kite can only rise against the wind." and finally last but not least, "It's not so much about the burden, but how you carry it."

God bless, and keep blessing....Niki C

HUAH!!!

Florida Governor Rick Scott signing in new laws against human trafficking. How humbling to look on and hear him honor the work STAAR Ministry had done.

For more information on how to have Niki speak at your church, school or organization, or to find out more about the ministry, please either:

E-mail: niki@staarministry.com

Go to: www.staarministry.com

Follow us on Facebook at STAAR Ministry or Like Daddy Used To Say

Made in the USA
Columbia, SC
18 January 2018